Research and Gender

Continuum Research Methods Series
Research Questions – Richard Andrews
Evaluation Methods in Research – Judith Bennett
Analysing Media Texts – Andrew Burn and David Parker
Action Research – Patrick Costello
Ethics in Research – Ian Gregory
Researching Post-compulsory Education – Jill Jameson and Yvonne Hillier
Systematic Reviews – Carol Torgerson
Using Focus Groups in Research – Lia Litosseliti

Real World Research Series
Developing a Questionnaire – Bill Gillham
The Research Interview – Bill Gillham
Case Study Research Methods – Bill Gillham

Questionnaire Design, Interviewing and Attitude Measurement – A. N. Oppenheim

Research and Gender

Liz Jones and Ian Barron

continuum

Continuum International Publishing Group
The Tower Building   80 Maiden Lane, Suite 704
11 York Road   New York
SE1 7NX   NY 10038

www.continuumbooks.com

British Library Cataloguing-in-Publication Data
A catalogue record for this book is available from the British Library.

ISBN 082648977X (paperback)

Library of Congress Cataloging-in-Publication Data
A catalog record for this book is available from the Library of Congress.

Typeset by YHT Ltd, London
Printed and bound in Great Britain by
Ashford Colour Press, Gosport, Hampshire.

Contents

Introduction

The principal aim of our book is to illustrate the relationship between gender and research. It does this by drawing upon the personal experiences of the two authors where their own gender and that of the research respondents is an integral area of study. Liz, for example, draws upon the experiences of working with 4-year-old children where a central aim of her research was aimed at understanding their part in the ways in which gender identities are constructed and played out within the nursery classroom. Specifically she questioned whether certain essentialist ways of being, including for example 'the tough male' or 'the passive female', could be avoided so that children could experience their gendered selves in multiple ways. However, by incorporating post-structuralist theories into the research, including practices of deconstruction, two important shifts occurred. First, the potential for behaving differently outside prescribed ways of being became a possibility. Second, Liz's own mindset that prompted habitual ways of behaving was destabilized and as a consequence a conceptual space was created where she could think differently about the 'performance' (Butler 1999) of gender as it is played out within the nursery classroom. This also included thinking about her own gendered performances.

Ian draws upon his experiences of research with 3–4-year-olds in a nursery school with an intake that is largely of Pakistani heritage. As the children, adults and environment interact in the diaspora space (Brah 1996) and practices of the nursery school, it becomes apparent that identities of gender, class, age and ethnicity are not separable and that they are revealed, shaped and reshaped in relation to the boundaries where different communities of practice (Lave and Wenger 1991) collide under the influence of factors such as power, religion and affluence. As attempts are made to broker the boundaries of existing communities of practice in order to find new ways forward and to reshape identities, there is a sense in which all that goes on in the nursery is a performance (Butler 1999). There is also a feeling that with essentialist identities revealed as inadequate in the face of fluidity of the enacted communities of practice, the script writer and the director both seem to be missing as old certainties are brought into the spotlight by the performance that is the research process.

Reflexivity is a key characteristic of both Liz's and Ian's work. As a consequence there are opportunities for the reader to appreciate some of the grapplings that have been undertaken by both as they sought to not only understand but additionally to document such claims to knowledge.

Writing this book has been important for two reasons. First, it has provided us with a forum in which to engage with the complexities that lie between the two sites of gender and research. Subsequently it will become more apparent how this engagement necessitated close scrutiny of our own values, ideologies and beliefs, including those located around feminism and social justice. Second, the discussions that have been spawned within the book will continue at the university where we both teach. We perceive this book as a tool – one that can be used to continue to open up debates, conversations and arguments about the interrelationship between gender and research.

Mapping the book

Chapter 1: The 'manliness' of research?

Here we chart some of the salient features of the Enlightenment project. Specifically we note the hierarchical nature of Enlightenment thought and its privileging of rationality, where men were identified with the rational and women with the irrational. Moreover, we mark out how the application of scientific reasoning could establish reliable truths about the real world and in this way objective mastery of reality could be achieved. Effectively, the task of creating knowledge was structured along gendered lines. Finally, we note two significant forms of resistance to Enlightenment thinking, that is, feminism and post-structuralism and how each has had an impact on our ways of making sense of the world.

Chapter 2: Researching gender: a feminist perspective

Very simply, to do feminist research is to put the social construction of gender at the centre of one's enquiry. Drawing on work undertaken in the nursery classroom where she was the teacher, Liz attempts to illustrate this process. She starts by elaborating on the issue. This centres on an example of play where the stereotypical roles that are assumed by both the girls and the boys cause Liz some disquiet – particularly when it is subjected to a feminist analysis. Overall the chapter illustrates the theoretical toings and froings that are undertaken where the onus is on the practitioner to develop 'better' practices in relation to more equitable gender relations.

Chapter 3: Researching gender: a postmodern perspective

There are some distinct similarities between post-modernism and feminism. As noted in Chapter 1, they both interrogate the inherent homocentric nature of all the fundamental dichotomies that have characterized Enlightenment reasoning and Western thinking generally. However, there are differences in the ways in which subjectivity/identity are understood. Feminism, for example, needs the subject of 'woman' in order to coalesce a politics of identity. Meanwhile, postmodernism interrogates notions of subjectivity and in so doing renders it fragmented and 'always in process'. However, Liz, in drawing on her own research, marks out certain repercussions, particularly the benefits when post-modernism is brought into a study that centres on gender.

Chapter 4: Researching gender: issues of masculinity

Attention now turns to the responses that have emerged to the impact of feminist perspectives on research. The chapter examines claims that feminism has promoted the interests and achievements of girls at the expense of those of boys and has caused a crisis in terms of male identity. While feminism generally espouses the values of the left and adopts critical perspectives in understanding gender identities, the new masculinism is more closely aligned with the right and with essentialist views. The new masculinism argues for 'natural' and biological differences between the genders, which it views as 'common sense', drawing upon biological determinist assertions that all aspects of identity are fixed and unchanging. Ian draws upon his own research, however, to examine the ways in which such perspectives do not provide for the nuances or the diaspora that are at the heart of all aspects of identity, and seeks to explore the value but also the difficulties in moving away from hegemonic identities.

Chapter 5: Undertaking research in a field that is feminized

This chapter considers in more depth the ways in which identities of gender, ethnicity and class are constantly negotiated and brokered within the economies of meaning that emerge from communities of practice. Through the experiences of carrying out research in a particular nursery school, Ian explores the relationship between the male researcher and the feminized environment in which he found himself. What seems to emerge is a form of multi-nodal identity trajectory where different aspects of identity are performed, negotiated and reflected upon in relation to each other and where difference and deferral are at the heart of what identity seems to involve. Consideration is given to the negotiation of identities among the children, between staff and children, between researcher and staff, between researcher and children and between researcher, staff and children, as Ian examines the ways in which he is positioned and positions himself among the nursery's communities of practice.

Chapter 6: Research as performance and practice

The final chapter seeks to explore the ways in which the carrying out of research may be conceptualized as involving a performance. The performance is enacted in the diaspora spaces at the boundary (Brah 1996) of ever-shifting patterns of behaviour and meaning-making in relation to the gender, ethnic, class and cultural dimensions of the performers and the context and under the operant discourses of power. The sense that can be made in any research situation is viewed as a representation of certain elements of that research context. This stance disturbs the parameters between which research is usually carried out and understood and 'is theorizing its own evolution as discontinuous, catastrophic, non-rectifiable, and paradoxical' (Lyotard 1984: 60). Ian argues that this does not mean that research is futile or meaningless but that the research process needs to involve providing an adequate account of the multiple and dynamic realities and identities which are enacted in order to seek out the sense and meanings that emerge from shifting performances which provide evidence of underlying explanatory tendencies (Bhaskar 1998a).

1

The 'Manliness' of Research?

If 'sawing off the branch on which one is sitting' seems foolhardy to men of common sense, it is not so for Nietzsche, Freud, Heidegger and Derrida; for they suspect that if they fall there is no ground to hit and that the most clear-sighted act may be a certain reckless sawing, a calculated dismemberment or deconstruction of the great cathedral-like trees in which Man has taken shelter for millennia (Culler 1982: 149).

Introduction

In this chapter our aim is to question whether research is gendered and if it is to consider how this has happened and whether it has any significance currently. We want to chart some of the philosophical movements that have underpinned and continue to influence how we both see and understand our social worlds and in so doing we want to demonstrate how these theories rest upon and draw strength from certain manifestations of what constitutes 'the subject'.

Our choice of title for this chapter endeavours to signal a number of things. First it is an attempt at nodding towards the Enlightenment project – the locus of the rational subject – that is man. For as Hekman notes, 'Since the Enlightenment, knowledge has been defined in terms of man, the subject, and espouses an

7

epistemology that is radically homocentric' (Hekman 1990: 8). This raises the question of whether in contemporary times this anthropocentric definition of knowledge still exists and if it does what might be the reverberations within present-day research circles.

Our second reason for the title centres on first considering whether there are certain characteristics that for a number of reasons have come to be thought of as 'manly' before moving to judge whether these impact on the ways in which research is 'performed'. Moreover, we try to fathom whose interests might be served or are served by such performances.

Thus we begin by dedicating some time to certain salient features that are the legacy of the Enlightenment. Specifically we draw attention to Positivism to illustrate both its debt to Enlightenment thinking and to highlight how it has contributed towards what Spivak refers to as 'mindset' (1980: 75), where particular ways of knowing and understanding the social world have become the basis for what could be described as common sense. We then move to draw an analogy between the phenomenon known as 'othering' and research where an appreciation of the former offers insights into the gendered nature of the latter. So by understanding how women have been 'othered' it is hoped that the reader might gain some purchase as to why research and some performances can first be considered as gendered and second why certain political interests seem to dictate a necessity for 'manly' ways. Finally we make clear the ways the Enlightenment inheritance has been resisted where post-structuralist theory has opened up possibilities for performing research in different ways.

Men of common sense

The cartoon-like image that Culler offers us with the quotation above provides a lovely metaphorical opening for discussing some of the core features of the Enlightenment. We will begin by considering 'men of common sense' for arguably it is men who because of their so-called sense – that is their capacity to be rational – constitute a central feature of the project. The Enlightenment project, or as some commentators refer to it, Modernity, was an intellectual movement that developed in England and Europe during the seventeenth and eighteenth centuries. Overall it was an intellectual quest to break with tradition, blind habit and slavish obedience to religious precepts and in its place secure a knowledge that was self-evident to reason and safe from all the demons of doubt. In other words the Enlightenment would lead society out of the darkness of irrationality and superstition that supposedly characterized the Middle Ages. 'Man' was no longer to be dependent on the guidance of 'another'. Rather by his own capacities he could progress. These 'capacities' included a faith that rational knowledge of society could be attained and that this knowledge was universal and thus objective. Knowledge that is required from the right use of reason is 'truth' in that it represents something real, unchanging and universal about the human mind and the structure of the natural world. Knowledge can be both neutral (that is grounded in universal reason, not particular 'interests') and socially beneficial. In other words, rational knowledge, because it is both rational and neutral, can lead to mental liberation and social betterment among humanity (McLennan 1992). Taylor summarizes the enterprise (1987: 42):

> When the subject totally comprehends the object and the object is perfectly reflected in the subject, the doubt and

uncertainty with which modern philosophy begins are finally overcome.

Given this line of thinking it is relatively easy to see why Kant (1724–1804), one of the most significant thinkers of the Enlightenment, saw this mental liberation in a kind of ages and stages way where man emerges from what Kant referred to as his 'self-imposed infancy', where infancy is being seen as an inability to use one's reason without the guidance of another. It is also possible to discern why progress as conceptualized within the Enlightenment project resonates with a 'root-tree' metaphor (Deleuze and Guattari 1987) where linear progress leads towards a 'better' life. Finally we can perhaps appreciate why critics have taken their own preferred choice of tool, be that post-structuralism or feminist theory, to undertake some reckless sawing as a 'strategic act of interruption of the methodological will to certainty and clarity of vision' (Stronach and MacLure 1997: 4). We will return to this issue subsequently.

Examining the ground

Modern man as a subject was therefore characterized as a living being capable of response, judgement and action on the world. In order to make judgements by necessity he had to be autonomous and coherent. Thus reason could be set to work to discover the underlying principles that govern nature and societies. Additionally language could be used unproblematically. As Flax writes (1990: 42):

> Just as the right use of reason can result in knowledge that represents the real, so, too, language is the medium in and through which such representation occurs. There is a

correspondence between word and thing (as between a correct truth claim and the real). Objects are not linguistically (or socially) constructed; they are merely made present to consciousness by naming and the right use of language.

It is these beliefs as outlined above that are the basis for many assumptions and serve as legitimation for contemporary Western culture. In brief, they have constituted Culler's 'cathedral-like trees' that have given 'Man ... shelter'.

Now while it is possible to see how within Enlightenment thinking generally 'man' and 'the rational subject' became synonymous, it is perhaps a little harder to extrapolate whether this phenomenon has any significance in relation to present-day research activities. One reason why the issue is of significance in relation to the possibilities of a research/gender nexus is that there is far greater emphasis placed on the 'doing' of research where the 'activities' of the business tend to create a forgetting of the philosophical underpinnings of research methodology. Scott and Usher elaborate further, 'An emphasis on the "doing" of research inevitably means an emphasis on methods and procedures, since these are in a sense the most obvious manifestations of the "doing" ... ' where what gets lost in all this activity is a 'consideration of the philosophical assumptions and issues with which "doing" is entangled' (1999: 1). Thus the general hustle and bustle of research where the pressure of getting the job done effectively renders philosophical considerations an extraneous, almost superfluous, pursuit. However, as Scott and Usher also note, while they might not be consciously considered, nevertheless both philosophical and epistemological issues are 'concealed' in the research process. Moreover this concealment comes both as a consequence of the busyness that we have already referred to but additionally it can be attributed to Positivism.

At a simple level Positivism is a philosophical position where the core belief is that certain and indubitable knowledge can be attained. In other words 'truth' can be established. The 'founding father' of Positivism, Comte, sought to develop positivist philosophy as a basis for the practice of modern science (Garratt and Li 2005) where Positivism could provide 'a powerful statement for the unity of all sciences and thus for the acceptability and necessity of employing the methods of the natural sciences in the study of social affairs' (Smith 1989: 40). As Parker notes, 'Positivism continues the narrative of the Enlightenment, telling a story of cultural progress in which modernity is depicted as the epoch when science finally replaces religion and custom as the foundation for social organization' (1997: 10).

With religion and custom sidelined men themselves were now placed in the position of having to grapple with epistemological issues that are located around the question 'How do we know what we think we know?' In the pursuit of 'knowledge' scientific reason was put to work and in so doing established a set of rules for 'knowing':

> By application of the rules, only certain kinds of knowledge would be considered valid; the rest would be refused that status ... Very quickly, the rules or grounds for this validity came to be found in the scientific method in the form of measurement, in testability and in the use of reason (Scott and Usher 1999: 11).

It is Positivism and its associated realist metaphysics that provide the basis or the foundations for our common-sense or habitual ways of thinking and it is for this reason – together with the overall busyness of 'doing' research – that there is a tendency not to stop in order to consider philosophical issues, including whether research might be gendered. So even when researchers are not working within a positivist paradigm, '[positivism] still exerts a powerful influence – an influence which considers reflexive questions to be both undesirable and unnecessary' (Scott and Usher 1999: 1). And if reflexive questions are omitted from the process then there will be an absence of inquiry in general about the philosophical underpinnings as well as an absence in specific matters such as whether the enterprise is 'gendered' or not.

Drawing an analogy between 'othering' and research: disturbing the ground

Above our efforts have been concerned with depicting certain salient features that emanated from the Enlightenment project and which still have immense impact on how we understand our social worlds. Additionally we have tried to highlight how Positivism, working within the spirit of the Enlightenment, seeks to use rational thinking as a means of establishing certainty. However, as the opening quotation indicates, the cathedral-like branches that have provided shelter have come under attack where various philosophers and a number of *isms* including feminism and post-structuralism have undertaken acts of radical pruning. Indeed it is not just branches that have been tampered with, it is the very ground which nurtures the tree that has been disturbed.

'Disturbing the ground' can be seen as work that is embarked on to dislocate the logic which support those binaries that have 'traditionally promised the comforts of certainty to philosophical thinking' (Stronach and MacLure 1997: 5), including for example rational/irrational and subject/object. The particular story that we want to tell in terms of 'resisting the inheritance' centres

13

on post-structuralist theory. As a first step we want to draw an analogy between a phenomenon known as 'othering' and 'doing research'. Drawing on Foucault (1972) we want to illustrate how specific discourses positioned woman as 'other' to men and in so doing we identify what some of the repercussions are when rationality gets used as a yardstick to normalize what it means 'to be' (MacLure 2003: 176). It is by understanding 'othering' and forms of resistance to it that the reader might gain some purchase as to why research can be considered as gendered where certain performances are undertaken in a 'manly' way for specific reasons.

'Othering'

The notion of 'other' has been of extreme inter-disciplinary interest for some considerable time. For example, the work of Simone de Beauvoir (1972) was located around a central thesis where woman is always 'Other' to man's 'Absolute'. She writes:

> Throughout history [women] have always been sub-ordinated to men; their dependency is not the result of an event or a change – it was not something that occurred. It is in part because it does not have the accidental character of a historical fact that otherness in this case appears as an absolute (1972: 24–5).

Meanwhile, Lacanian psychoanalysis has directed attention at how subjectivity is produced in language where 'othering' (inevitably) occurs. As Grosz (1990) describes it, Lacan perceives the phallus as the 'Master' signifier where such privileging of the masculine is nigh on impossible to dislodge. So, the 'feminine situation' is not just characterized by a refusal of certain rights or privileges. Rather, it is because access to the very language in which those rights are expressed is denied her:

> Without a phallus, without a name, the female subject will always be in question, always have to find its identity in something else, will always hover on the edge of non-existence (Nye 1988: 140).

Additionally, Foucault's (1972) analysis of discourse where the emphasis is on 'practices that form the objects of which they speak' (p. 49) has had significant influence on how we ourselves understand 'othering'. In isolating 'disciplinary power' Foucault demonstrates how whole populations and the individual and his or her body can be regulated. Briefly, the aim of disciplinary power is to bring the

> lives, deaths, activities, work, miseries and joys of the individual as well as his/her physical health, sexual practices and family life under stricter discipline and control; bringing to bear on them the power of administrative regimes, the expertise of the professional, and the knowledge provided by the 'disciplines' of the social sciences. Its basic object is to produce a human body who can be treated as a docile body (Dreyfus and Rabinow 1982: 135).

It is through 'discourses' that disciplinary power circulates. Within a Foucaldian approach, discourses are inextricably linked to social institutions including for example the law, church, education and family as well as to the disciplines that both regularize and normalize the conduct of those who are brought within the compass of those institutions. If we look back to the nineteenth century it is possible to discern how a discourse such as medicine was used to legitimate both colonialism and slavery. Accordingly within the precepts of the discourse African people were not only considered biologically suited to slavery, additionally, as were women, they were scientifically categorized as irrational and therefore unsuited for the task of self-government (Stanton 1960; Brah 1996). As Weedon (1999: 9) highlights:

> scientific racism and similar work on gender set the terms of the debates about difference well into the twentieth century. Indeed, the negative qualities consistently attributed to sexual and racial difference from a white, middle class male norm by the institutions of science, medicine, philosophy and the law made it very difficult to see questions of difference in positive terms.

Effectively discourses have the capacity to not only regulate what is 'normal' but equally be exclusionary. Judith Butler's (1993) work follows a similar trajectory in examining the relationship between 'bodies' and 'othering' where there are bodies that 'matter' while others are 'abject'. This process of separating out or excluding is a deliberate strategy where it is directed to particular kinds of others and is as a consequence hegemonic or, in other words, '[it] proclaims the beliefs and indeed, the subjectivity of a dominant group as the only true or valid ones, precisely by excluding certain others as beyond reason or humanity' (MacLure 2003: 41). Gee (1990) emphasizes how these practices transcribe into commonsense or taken-for-granted notions of 'the right ways to think, feel and behave' (p. xx). Through discursive power, understandings about 'what counts as normal (and deviant) sorts of human beings, as well as what counts as normal (and deviant) relationships between them' (Gee 1990: xi) would be prescribed. Di Stefano (1990) captures the overall state of play. She writes:

> we are just beginning to understand the heretofore suppressed feminine dimensions of public and private life; and

that what has passed as gender neutral vocabulary of reason, morality, cognitive development, autonomy, justice,
history, theory, progress and enlightenment is imbued with
masculine feeling (p. 64).

Thus the rules of discourse allow certain people to be
subjects of statements and others to be objects.

By charting out some of the underpinning mechanisms
that constitute 'othering' we have hopefully demonstrated how rationality in a general sense has been played
out where the yardstick that has dictated what it means 'to
be' centres on the male subject. As the book unfolds it
will become evident how feminists at various junctures in
history have challenged the Enlightenment legacy. For
now we want to turn to post-structuralist theory where in
various ways the logic underpinning Enlightenment
thinking has been put under pressure. Additionally, by
drawing on an example of research activity in which Liz
was involved, we want to try to illustrate how the power of
rationality was evoked for particular reasons, where masculinist practices predisposed a particular performance in
terms of Liz's practice. The question of 'How might
things be different?' is then considered.

Chopping off branches

In brief, the work of post-structuralist theory can be
characterized as a relentless attack on the 'certainty' of
Enlightenment philosophical thinking where the challenge has been and continues to be sustained erosion on
dichotomous thinking. Thus it is those binary oppositions, which as we have already noted have 'traditionally
promised the comforts of certainty to philosophical
thinking', that post-structuralism confronts. Such work
does not ignore these binaries, nor does it attempt to

transcend them, rather it is work that 'complicates' the relations between them (Stronach and MacLure 1997: 7). So for example following Derrida (1976) a number of post-structuralist theorists (e.g. Lather 1991; Parker 1997; Stronach and MacLure 1997; Brown and Jones 2001; MacLure 2003) have incorporated deconstruction into their work. In undertaking a deconstructive reading of a text (and it has to be remembered that this word is 'stretched' within such enquiries to include writing, language, film, advertisements as well as educational practice) the task is to

> turn the rationality expressed by or implicit within the text back upon itself to take apart its rational structure ... one would first expose and describe the rational system; then assault it ... No matter how strong the logic, how tight the reasoning, deconstruction operates like a virus on the text's immune system, turning its logic against itself (Parker 1997: 71).

As an example let us examine the following that has been extracted from a UK policy document, *Excellence in Schools* (DfEE 1997: 14–16):

> Investment in learning in the 21st century is the equivalent of investment in the machinery and technical innovation that was essential in the first great industrial revolution. Then it was physical capital; now it is human capital ... We know that children who benefit from nursery education – especially from disadvantaged backgrounds – are more likely to succeed in primary school ... Our aim is that all children should begin school with a head start in literacy, numeracy and behaviour, ready to learn and make the most of primary.

Because of discourses that are in circulation currently in the UK a statement such as this seems on the face of it simply to echo what has entered into our collective consciousness as 'common sense' in relation to children and their schooling. But a deconstructive reading takes note of the way in which the knowledge/power nexus is capitalized upon to mark out children as separate, deficient and incomplete (Walkerdine 1984). Children are positioned as being outside of those who know – they are excluded from the 'we'. That said it is an exclusion that can be remedied. Success or progress will occur, but in order for this to happen children – particularly those from 'disadvantaged backgrounds' – will have to be regulated – not only for their own good but also as a social 'investment'. So while the above programme is clearly predicated on notions of 'progress' it nevertheless works from a premise where 'the knowledge that is part of the lives of younger human beings has been judged as either non-existent or of poor quality' (Cannella and Viruru 2004: 88). In order to become rational or put slightly differently, to have a 'head start', children have to be made 'ready' – a process that cannot be left to chance but is regulated through specific linear stages of advancement. In summary, what this extract encapsulates is a process whereby human beings are positioned on a continuum between those who know, and who are accordingly more advanced, and those who do not know, that is the ignorant. Moreover it is a *singular* story about progress that is predicated on a universal truth both about 'the child' and 'education'. It is by knitting together a number of binaries including those of adult/child, advantaged/disadvantaged and capital/poverty – where one side of the binary is given substance and rendered positive by its negative 'other' – that the above statement above acquires its logic.

'Manly' performances

So in *practice* what kinds of performance would be enacted if the assumptions upon which habitual ways of 'doing' research were eroded? What is possible once 'neutrality, objectivity, observable facts, transparent description, clean separation of the interpreter and the interpreted ... are called into question?' (Lather 1991: 105). How can we positively 'know' when these basic concepts have been disrupted?

In order to address these questions we turn now to research that Liz undertook when working in an inner-city school in the north-west of England. The research was part of her doctorial studies where one of the aims of the project was to incorporate action research so that she could both monitor her own professional practice and use it to bring about changes for the better. Liz wanted to employ action research to achieve an 'ideal', which in her case centred on developing a classroom context where there were more equitable gender relations. Now while such an aim appears on the surface to be straightforward Liz had added a *complication* into her study. She had become embroiled in post-structuralist theory where as a consequence the rationale that supports an activity such as action research – where a core feature is the reflective teacher – is sorely tested because the latter works from the assumption that one can use reason, clarity and truth to progress (Barry 1995). However, rather than abandoning the enterprise the study sought to incorporate post-structuralism in order to interrogate this assumption as well as Liz's own investment in notions such as 'equitable gender relations'.

Here, however, rather than focusing on 'gender relations' – an area that will be troubled in other chapters – we want to elaborate on an 'ordinary' instance that Liz recorded in her research journal where a 4-year-old boy is unable to write his own name independently.

Our example centres on a young child, Andrew, who despite being given sundry opportunities for learning had not mastered the skill of writing his own name unaided. So while aged only 4 nevertheless, within the context of early years education in the UK, there were a number of factors which had already been established where the expected outcome in terms of Andrew's learning was that he *should* be able to perform this task. For example, during the course of his nursery education Andrew's progress was constantly monitored, evaluated and recorded. Careful observations were undertaken where evidence was collected that identified Andrew's development as commensurate with the norm. Other artefacts such as samples of his drawings substantiated this judgement. Thus in his learning portfolio there were examples of his very early attempts at drawing a figure that were just random scribbles to more recent sophisticated efforts which were much more representative of a human figure, including closely observed details such as five fingers being ascribed to each hand. These provided a means for charting his developing competence and as a somewhat crude guide to his inherent abilities.

What became apparent to Liz when reflecting on her practice in relation to Andrew was that despite her rational approach Andrew had not attained the specified outcome which in this instance was writing his name independently. Notwithstanding the fact that Andrew's development had been 'monitored', 'evaluated' and 'recorded' he nevertheless had failed to achieve. Despite Liz's efficiency and the overall bureaucratization of Andrew's early education an aspect of his learning had foundered. So while constant surveillance and inspection had been undertaken the desired outcome had not been secured.

Liz's position could be described as that of the technical–rationalist (Siegel 1988) where 'efficient means' *should* have secured an end. In effect Liz's teaching in relation to Andrew is a performance that is ensnared within a positivist paradigm. It would appear from the above vignette that she holds a teleological view of education where 'actions are to be judged or valued according to the extent to which they are effective in bringing about whatever are taken to be education's proper ends' (Parker 1997: 11). By holding a perception of learning as linear, Liz's task as Andrew's teacher was to put reason to work so as to find the most effective means of securing the 'end'. In this instance Liz's notion of professionalism 'consists in instrumental problem solving made rigorous by the application of scientific theory and technique' (Schön 1983: 2). In our view her performance is supported by and given sustenance by the masculinist notion of rationality that has previously been described.

In brief Liz was left with a sense of deficit; somewhere along the 'line' of Andrew's learning she had been remiss and consequently he was left unable to meet the challenge imposed by the regulation of the 'norm'. Situated as she was with an action research cycle where the onus is on her to confront, analyse and develop her practice Liz was clearly left with a problem. Having identified the problem the rational response would be to identify where the weakness was in Andrew's learning, which of course would necessitate Liz ascertaining gaps in her teaching. Such a step would contribute towards Liz becoming a better and more effective teacher. But there is cause for pause in these assumptions. In her preoccupations with Andrew's learning Liz had to recognize both a 'disappointment' in relation to her performance as the rational teacher and with herself as the rational agent within action research where both have a 'commitment to the authority of reason' (Parker 1997: 32). So while action research might be averse to a 'means–end' conception of rationality it nevertheless still has at its core the rational and autonomous subject. This 'disappointment' stemmed from and was fuelled by Liz's entanglements with post-structuralist theories where as we have already noted there is an extreme scepticism of this particular version of 'subjectivity'.

Concluding remarks

However, while all these perambulations might work at foregrounding the manliness of research the reader might want to ask, quite rightly, 'But where does this leave Andrew?' What about his problem?

First let us try and establish whether there is a problem. Parker (1997: 41) makes the following point about 'problem setting' when he writes:

> [it] is the construction of a perspective on a situation the description of which precipitates anomalies. Problems in turn are parasitic for their existence on the chosen descriptions; they are, we might say theory relative; and the adoption of a different theory – a different paradigm – will have the result of some problems being dissolved whilst others are created.

Scheurich (1997: 114) makes a not too dissimilar point:

> how social problems are named, defined and discussed is a social process and that social visibility of some 'problems' as social problems and the invisibility of other 'problems' as social problems ... is also part of this process of social construction.

Thus the research activity that was undertaken in relation to Andrew and his learning was situated within systems of scientific ideas. In this instance these were drawn from bodies of knowledge concerned with child development in general and developmental psychology in particular. It is these that allowed Liz to assess whether Andrew's learning is progressing along a specific trajectory. Overall the school curriculum inscribes rules and standards by which reason is constructed where, 'The rules and standards produce social technologies whose consequences are regulatory' (Popkewitz 1997: 145). Similarly Liz in trying to 'make sense' of Andrew is also situated in regulatory practices that predispose her to 'see' the world in particular ways. Within the classroom she has to construct knowledge about Andrew as a prerequisite of acting intentionally. As we have noted it is the notion of the rational subject that underpins the theory that encompasses Andrew, Liz and 'the problem'. How then might this problem be reframed? How might things be different paradigmatically?

One point of departure could be to mount a sustained attack on our commonplace research activities where for example we describe and categorize young children and their families. As noted earlier the busyness of research can overshadow other pressing matters including the systemic violence that can unwittingly be directed at those who for whatever reason fall outside of regulated ideas of what it means 'to be'. Additionally we can reconsider certain metaphors that have traditionally been used to capture knowledge. Andrew's story for instance could be understood as a representation of a modernist model for knowledge where 'careful nurturing of the roots will favour strong growth' (Jones *et al.* 2005: 205). But can a 'root-tree' metaphor be sustained in a world that has witnessed profound changes? Is it an adequate means for capturing the social fragmentation in which young lives such as Andrew's are lived out? For some (e.g. Lather 1991; Brown and Jones 2001; Jones *et al.* 2005) the rhizome has supplanted the modernist notion of 'growth' because of its capacity to grow in extraordinary ways:

Rhizomes defy the regularity of linear growth. They do not have a central or main trunk. Nor do they emerge from a single shoot. Instead with their underground stems and aerial roots, they upset all pre-conceptions that are brought to notions of growth (Brown and Jones 2001: 179).

Overall reframing 'the problem' necessitates the need to decentre the rational subject. As Popkewitz notes (1997: 150), 'The decentring of the subject has its own sense of irony: there is an acceptance of the need to construct knowledge that can enable people to act intentionally'. However, he goes on to note how this has to occur in a different location 'than that argued in the philosophy of consciousness'. Undertaking research outside the parameters of the philosophy of consciousness means asking hard and pressing questions about those framing mechanisms (Lather 1991) that stipulate what we see and how we see it. In this way the rational subject that gives licence to certain acts of manly research is made into an 'insistent contest and resignification' (Butler 1993: 7) not as a foundation of research that is taken as the unquestionable.

2

Researching Gender: A Feminist Perspective

> The man who fights for two or more in the struggle for existence, who has all the responsibility and the cares of tomorrow, who is constantly active in combating the environment and human rivals, needs more brain than the woman he must protect and nourish, than the sedentary woman, lacking any interior occupations, whose role is to raise children, love and be passive (Topinard 1888: 22, quoted in Gould 1981: 104).

Introduction

Patti Lather writes, 'Very simply, to do feminist research is to put the social construction of gender at the centre of one's inquiry' (1991: 71). Becky Francis (2001) breaks this down into four central tenets: a concern with gender; a perception of women as generally disadvantaged in gender relations; a perception of this gender inequity as problematic and a consequent aim to emancipatory reform. In this chapter in drawing on Liz's research the aim is to illustrate the 'doing' of feminist research where the complexities of gender and the ways in which it is performed lie at the heart of the enquiry.

The opening quotation marks out vividly nineteenth-century assumptions concerning men and women. These were grounded in a mixture of biology plus nineteenth-century middle-class views of masculinity and femininity. Weedon (1999) argues that these assumptions are still very much with us today and are reflected in numerous examples of popular culture. Think here of the endless 'superhero' portrayals that are featured on children's television channels where for example Batman saves his city from evil – a task that always includes rescuing several women. Meanwhile endless adult-oriented films draw upon the goody/baddy narrative where the good guys vanquish the bad, where women are mainly decorative, passive and submissive and effectively become a reward for the good guys' brave endeavours. The Bond movies are representative of this particular genre.

Gender difference is socially constructed and hence 'is an effect of relations of knowledge and power which permeates all areas of life' (Weedon 1999: 5). Yelland and Grieshaber (1998) note that gender is a process which begins at birth and is continually being shaped, moulded and reshaped throughout life. For Liz in her capacity as a teacher of young children and working from a feminist perspective this development carries a set of implications where there are possibilities to 'cut into' procedures in order to develop and sustain equitable gender relations within the classroom. As noted it is aspects of this research that provide the basis for this chapter.

As a starting point we draw on an example of play that was recorded by Liz in her research journal. This was a research tool that was never far from Liz when she was at work. Here anecdotes that centred on the children's play and their conversations with one another as well as those with Liz were hurriedly recorded. Such observations then became the basis for analysis and theorizing. This chapter aims to show some of the repercussions when a feminist framework is brought to the analysis of the data. It must be stressed however that it is not our intention to offer a comprehensive guide to feminist thinking. Rather, our efforts are directed at showing how different perspectives provided different locations for Liz to view gender that then served to orient her practice in particular ways. We turn immediately to the example before moving to offer a number of readings.

An example of play

The setting for this story is the 'Home Corner'.[1] Jane has dressed herself in a motley collection of clothes from the dressing-up box. She is trying to spoon-feed Jessica, another girl aged 4. Jessica has her mouth firmly clamped against Jane's attempts to get the spoon into her mouth.

> Jane: *If you don't eat all your food I'll go mad.*
> Jane: *You'll go to bed if you don't eat it all up.*
> Jessica still shows no sign of opening her mouth.
> Jane: *Right . . . I'll need this bag for my shopping. Looks as if I'll need my coat.*
> Jane takes Jessica by the hand and leads her out of the Home Corner into the main body of the room. Two 4-year-old boys charge at the girls. Both boys have their arms stuck out straight in front of them – a pose that they have copied from the Superman character.
> Michael: *We're the police. You're under arrest.*
> Jane: *You've got the wrong ones. We've done nothing wrong.*
> The boys lowered their arms and went off to play elsewhere. Jane and Jessica return to the Home Corner where Jane declares, *Right . . . it's bed-time.*

What is a woman?

Women may be capable of education, but they are not made for the most advanced sciences, for philosophy and certain forms of artistic production which require universality. Women may have ideas, taste, and elegance but they do not have the ideal. The difference between men and women is like that between animals and plants; men correspond to animals, while women correspond to plants because their life is a more placid unfolding, the principle of which is the undetermined unity of feeling. When women hold the helm of government, the state is at once in jeopardy, because women regulate their actions not by the demands of universality, but by arbitrary inclination and opinions (Hegel, cited in Le Doeuff 1991: 109).

In the previous chapter considerable energy went into exploring how the Enlightenment project, Modernity, focused on 'man' as the rational, unified and autonomous subject. Understandably feminism in its various guises and at different historical junctures has challenged this version of subjectivity. However, while it is understandable that feminists have sought and continue to confront the fundamental assumptions of the modernist legacy, there have nevertheless been extreme difficulties reconsidering who or what is a 'woman'. For feminism 'woman' is a central concept because it is 'the necessary point of departure for any feminist theory and politics' but that said it is highly problematic because as a category 'it is crowded with the over determinations of male supremacy, invoking in every formulation the limit, contrasting Other, or mediated self-reflection of a culture built on the control of females' (Alcoff 1988: 405).

What follows traces some of Liz's perambulations where she too took as her departure point the category of 'woman'. Specifically her efforts were directed at unravelling Jane's evocations of 'womanly performances'. Her unravellings were prompted in part by an anxiety that the kinds of play that the children were enacting worked at hardening stereotypical assumptions of what it means to be male and female. Should Jane for example be encouraged or deterred in her play? So while Jane is clearly adroit at being able to convey some of the embedded intricacies of being a mother, isn't there a feminist necessity to broaden the girls' horizons, to question their seeming dependence on an age-old narrative of what it means to be a woman? But what does it mean to be a woman?

Feminist responses

There are stark similarities between Hegel and Topinard's version of what it means to be a 'woman'. Both men emphasize the passivity of women and both allude to women's inabilities for 'advanced' thinking. In Liz's nursery considerable energy had gone into ensuring that the classroom environment was structured in such ways as to ensure that the children – girls especially – could 'experience' gender in ways that disputed these sedimented assumptions held by Hegel and Topinard, and which have left indelible traces on what it means to be a boy/girl and a woman/man in contemporary times. Hence in the classroom the children's learning materials, including the books that were read to them and those they accessed independently, had been selected because they were free of traditional sex–role stereotypes. All the children had equal opportunities to access all learning materials. In brief Liz's classroom (like numerous other early years classrooms) was benefiting from and actively pursuing equity work which was inspired by research activities where a central ambition was to ensure that education in general was non-sexist. Overall, and to hugely simplify, feminist scholarship within education in the late 1970s and early 1980s focused on, first, identifying the ways in which boys dominated classrooms and, second, how this could be minimized. So it was found that boys took up more physical space and teacher attention both inside classrooms and when outside playing (Clarricoates 1978; Walkerdine 1981; Spender 1982; May and Ruddock 1983; Askew and Ross 1988). There was also disquiet in the ways in which the curriculum that was followed within schools communicated bias. Scott (1980) for instance surveyed all textbooks in a London comprehensive school and identified that not only did the majority enhance the image of men (at the expense of women) but that they frequently presented a distorted representation of the world which was even more sexist than the real world (pp. 114–15).

Within the specific site of early years it was noted that young boys accessed and used construction materials more readily than girls and moreover were less prepared to work collaboratively on tasks. Girls meanwhile were prepared to share so that through group effort a project such as a tall tower could materialize (Davis and Tichner 1986).

In Liz's practice 'girls-only' play sessions with construction materials had been initiated as a way of provoking greater gender equity where the girls might have opportunities to experience and improve upon skills that would allow them more confidence and competence in mathematics and science – subjects that were perceived as male oriented. A link had been made between competences in each of these and such play (MacNaughton *et al.* 1986; Skelton and Hall 2001). Not too surprisingly Liz had also undertaken steps to encourage the girls to get themselves involved in 'non-traditional' role-play and it was in part because she had invested considerable energies in this that she found herself perplexed by the play of Jane and her 'baby'. For it seemed that while certain structural changes had been made one particular story about what it means to be a woman was 'fixed'.

Liberal feminism

There are of course direct links between Liz's liberal feminist practices and those undertaken by eighteenth- and nineteenth-century first-wave feminists including Mary Wollstonecraft and Harriet Taylor. Both Wollstonecraft and Taylor in borrowing from liberal and democratic theory sought civil rights on the same basis as men. So just as the likes of Locke, Rousseau and Bentham were arguing for all men to be equal similar arguments were being articulated on behalf of women. For instance Mary Wollstonecraft's *A Vindication of the Rights of Woman* (1792/1975) stressed the importance of education where, quite simply, women should be educated as men were. Nye (1988: 12) offers us this abridged version of Wollstonecraft's vision:

> They [women] should read philosophy, logic and mathematics. They should be encouraged to exercise; whatever physical weaknesses they possess should be overcome, not magnified. When they are afraid, they should not be cuddled but should be called cowards. In this way, women will become economically independent and fully capable of political participation.

Similarly more than half a century later Harriet Taylor (1807–58) in conjunction with John Stuart Mill (1806–73) was still arguing the same points, but universal suffrage had been added to the argument. In brief, they argued that women should be granted all political privileges, including the vote and the right to run for public office. Furthermore they should also have the choice of being able to work rather than to marry and to receive an education that would allow for such an ambition to materialize. In this way women would then be on equal footing to men. As we have said, there are parallels between these sets of demands and aspirations and those that were being practised by Liz and other feminist teachers.

Cultural feminism: Jane's play a cause for celebration?

If we return to the children's play we can see that Jane is highly practical. Although not seemingly adept at feeding her child she nevertheless is able to organize herself and her baby so that coats are put on, bags collected and shopping undertaken. Additionally she is able to cross the divide between pragmatism and logic by using sound argument to rebuff the boys, that is, it is nonsense to arrest her because, as she put it, '*You've got the wrong ones. We've done nothing wrong*'. So while it is evident that Jane favoured a particular type of play (where she drew upon her perceptions of domestic life in general but mothering in particular) has she not also indicated that she is a clever individual who can use her own knowledge of the world in order to outwit the boys? Metaphorically has she not achieved something of a feminist victory where the robust play of the boys was foiled by her quiet but purposeful understanding of the ways of the world? In brief does it matter that on some occasions Jane wants to slip into this role and play at keeping house? Is there something 'wrong' with the play and, if there is, in what way could it be 'corrected' and set to rights?

Mention has been made of type of play. Effectively it was making clear in Liz's own mind the difference between *type* and *stereotype* that triggered further troubling thoughts where further excursions were made into feminist thinking. To expand: Jane was demonstrating and using certain characteristics which enabled all of us present, that is children and adults alike, to classify her first as 'a woman' and second as 'a mother'. Similarly the boys in their guise were manifestations of the epitome of maleness – the superhero. As a tactic we all make sense of the world by classifying it into *types* where we 'understand the world by referring individual objects, people or events in our heads to the general classificatory schemes into which – according to our culture – they fit' (Hall 1997: 257). Broadly speaking 'a type is any simple, vivid, memorable, easily grasped and widely recognized characterization in which a few traits are foregrounded and change or "development" is kept to a minimum' (Dyer 1977: 28). Meanwhile stereotyping takes these 'simple, vivid, memorable, easily grasped and widely recognized' characteristics and reduces individuals so that they become the sum parts of these. In other words they are essentialized where identity becomes rigidly fixed. Clearly if we look back at the Hegel and Topinard quotations it is possible to see that this is precisely what both were doing. Thus women are 'other' to men, where because they 'correspond to plants' and are as a consequence inherently 'placid' they are unequal to the task of government. Similarly Mary Wollstonecraft's vision rested on exchanging one set of characteristics for another. Thus women in order to become equal had to expunge all that deemed them women so as to become 'like men'. That is via education women could enter certain male preserves so that they too could become logical, philosophical and mathematical. Additionally exercises would work at making them fit, strong and manly. In brief women would exchange one essentialist position for another.

A cultural feminists' perspective of Jane's play (Rich 1976; Daly 1978) might lead Liz to argue that Jane in her play is merely capitalizing on her 'bond with the natural order' (Rich 1976: 21) where the care of her 'baby' could be understood as a natural necessity born out of a natural need and moreover she is demonstrating – as she so clearly is – 'womanly expertise'. Indeed it is a line of thinking that can be and has been used to valorize the position of women as carers because they are 'full of superior virtues and values, to be credited and learned from rather than despised' (Alcoff 1988: 414). So on the one hand cultural feminists have championed women and their (so-called) natural attributes. However, while it is one thing to valorize positive attributes such as caring, nurturing, shopping and cooking there is nevertheless a danger that in doing so an essentialist notion of 'womanhood' is reinforced. For, as Alcoff points out, these very attributes have been honed out of necessity. She writes (1988: 414):

> Under conditions of oppression and restrictions on freedom of movement, women, like other oppressed groups, have developed strengths and attributes that should be correctly credited, valued and promoted.

But she also warns that there is a danger that such a position 'reinforces essentialist explanations of these attributes' and as a consequence solidifies 'the belief in an innate "womanhood"' to which women must adhere 'lest they be deemed either inferior or not "true" women' (Alcoff 1988: 414). So while Liz found herself crediting Jane because of her skills and additionally she knew that she would continue to use resources and so on that attempted to eradicate negative versions of femininity she nevertheless recognized that she was only operating along one track, one which did not destabilize a unitary and essentialist version of what it means to be either a girl or a boy. Additionally it was a track where both social class and race was ignored.

Social class and race

It is perhaps possible to locate in Jane's play an awareness of what it means to be a mother on limited economic resources. Jane, as were the other children in the nursery, was growing up in an area of Manchester where lives are blighted by unemployment, crime is prevalent and institutions such as the family are splintered. So perhaps given this backcloth her frustrations over her child refusing to eat might well have been born out of insights into what it means to raise children where faddyness in terms of eating is difficult to tolerate because of limited economic resources, which of course impacts upon emotional tolerance to cope with the seeming intransigence of the child. What therefore had to be recognized was that Jane was not only performing as a woman but additionally her social class informed her act. In recognizing this Liz was obliged to confront the question of whether the patriarchal gender relations manifest in the children's play when lived out for 'real' would then be instrumental in maintaining and reproducing the social relations of capitalism. Indeed many of the mothers of the children of the nursery had 'caring' jobs where for low wages they looked after the elderly and/or the disabled, cleaned houses, fostered children or offered child-minding services in their own homes. Of course such activities were on top of the unpaid work that they performed on a daily basis as 'the wife', or 'the lone parent' and 'the mother'. So while these women (and indeed Jane) are capitalizing upon and trading skills that are embedded within their performance of being women they are simultaneously being exploited (Skeggs 1997; Jones and Osgood 2006).

Moreover it would appear that in setting up an essentialized notion of what it means to be a woman an attempt was being made to speak for all, including women of colour, lesbians, differently abled women and so on. As

Lather (1991: 29) succinctly notes, 'the work of women of color (for example, Lorde 1984; Smith 1983; hooks 1984; Moraga and Anzaldua 1983: Lugones and Spellman 1983; Lugones 1987) documents resistance to the universalizing tendencies of feminist theorizing, resistance that grew out of a desire not for better theory but for survival'.

So for Liz, while on the one hand she welcomed those efforts that sought to offset the systematic denigration of women that is inherently embedded in patriarchy, she was nevertheless becoming increasingly sceptical of feminist accounts that rested on essentialist notions of what it means to be a woman. Similarly, while acknowledging an attraction to the idea of practising forms of representation outside patriarchal colonization (Weedon 1999), where for example Hélène Cixous' theory of feminine writing offers a challenge to the patriarchal symbolic order (Cixous 1987), she was still confused about whether this arose from a *natural* disposition where women have modes of expression that are inherently different to men. However, what she was becoming increasingly interested in was whether the girls in her class could use existing language in order to resist patriarchal forms of subjectivity. Her interests did not lie in the direction of girls 'being like boys' where through the symbolic order they could demonstrate sets of traits traditionally associated with what it is to be male (and vice versa). Rather, she was concerned to develop a capacity in all the children for critical thinking.

It may be recalled that Jane was able to resist 'the police' by calling upon a logic that was immediately recognizable to the boys. That is the rules stipulating who may or may not be arrested were premised on whether an individual has or has not done something 'wrong'. So in this particular situation the boys and girls alike acknowledged some notion of justice. Progressively it became Liz's ambition to develop a pedagogy that encouraged her class to become critical of those ways in which social structures were coercive with reference to gender relations. In brief, Liz aspired to promoting a 'theoretical space for creating a discourse capable of raising new questions, offering oppositional practices and producing fresh objects of analysis' (Giroux 1991: 501). Boler's (1999) 'pedagogy of discomfort' is situated within a similar vein where the onus is on collaborative critical enquiry. Here teachers and students alike engage in critical enquiry regarding values and cherished beliefs and to 'examine constructed self-images in relation to how one has learned to perceive others' (p. 116). What might then emerge is a 'counter hegemony' that Weiler (1988: 52) defines as:

> the creation of a self-conscious analysis of a situation and the development of collective practices and organization that can oppose the hegemony of the existing order and begin to build the base for a new understanding and transformation.

There is an obvious political impetus in such work where as a first step there must be recognition of how a category such as 'woman' has been shaped specifically by the dominant culture of a particular moment. Certainly attributes such as caring should be valued and promoted. But as noted previously what must be shunned are those controlled and limiting circumstances that gave rise to the attributes (Alcoff 1988). Alcoff elaborates further (p. 415):

> the problem with the cultural feminist response to sexism is that it does not criticise the fundamental mechanism of oppressive power used to perpetuate sexism and in fact reinvokes that mechanism in its supposed solution.

Her reference to 'the mechanism of power' draws upon the work of Foucault (1983) where according to his account the construction of subjectivity is situated within a discourse where knowledge and power are inextricably woven into a coercive structure so that it 'forces the individual back on himself [sic] and ties him to his own identity in a constraining way' (p. 212). Given this view homogenized and essentialist formulations of what it means to be a woman 'tie' or fix the individual to her identity as a woman and thus cannot serve as a pro-gramme for change in gender relations.

A consideration of Jane's play outside essentialism

In yet another perambulation Liz turned to Julia Kriste-va's essay 'Women's Time' (1981) as a way of working her way out of what seemed like a theoretical cul-de-sac. According to Kristeva in order for feminism to develop further it has to take on board the task of problematizing the term 'woman'. She expands (p. 193):

> I think that the apparent coherence which the term 'woman' assumes in contemporary ideology, apart from its 'mass' or 'shock' effect for activists' purposes, essentially has the negative effect of effacing the differences among the diverse functions or structures which operate beneath this word.

Thus the term 'woman' fails in Kristeva's view to capture the complexities that characterize female subjectivity. This is not to say she is against feminism. On the contrary she credits the various women's movements with 'ren-dering painful' (ibid: 195) the situation of women and working to eradicate social anomalies. Additionally, while recognizing that socialism together with feminism have

39

contributed to the quality of women's lives, both have nevertheless failed to eradicate sexism. As a consequence for Kristeva 'the struggle is no longer concerned with the quest for equality but, rather, with difference and specificity' (ibid: 196). Thus what the 'new generation' of feminists have to confront is the *symbolic* question. She writes:

> Sexual difference – is at once biological, physiological and relative to reproduction – is translated by and translates a difference in the relationship of subjects to the symbolic contract which *is* the social contract: a difference then in the relationship to power, language and meaning (p. 196, author's emphasis).

Having directed our attention to the symbolic order she then asks 'what can be our [i.e. woman's] place in the symbolic contract?' (ibid: 198). In other words how can women create a space within the symbolic order in order to transform it? Kristeva argues that the feminist struggle must be seen politically and historically as a three-tiered one. First, women must not give up on the struggle for equal access to the social order. So, retaining the category 'woman' is useful in maintaining the struggle to secure equity. However, Kristeva expresses caution about the mix between women and notions of power. Her concern is that while women have assumed executive, industrial and cultural power, this has not radically altered the nature of power, which is still resolutely hegemonic. Thus while she feels that women should continue to demand access into the social order, work should also be done to transform the nature of power. In Kristeva's view women must make attempts to avoid and detach themselves from centralized power so that through their 'critical, differential and autonomous interventions women can render decision making institutions more flexible' (p. 202).

Second, it still remains politically essential for feminists to defend women as women in order to counteract the patriarchal oppression that precisely despises women *as* women. However she does warn against feminism establishing itself as a counter-culture. She writes:

> As with any society, the counter society is based on the expulsion of an excluded element, a scapegoat charged with the evil of which the community duly constituted can then purge itself ... Modern protest movements have often reiterated this logic, in capital alone, in the other religion, in the other sex. Does not feminism become a kind of inverted sexism when this logic is followed to its conclusion? (p. 202).

In other words – and this is Kristeva's third strategy – feminism must take into account the *metaphysical* nature of gender identities. Not to do so runs the risk of both using and 'taking over the very metaphysical categories set up by patriarchy in order to keep women in their places' (Moi 1985: 13). So if the very dichotomy man/woman as an opposition may be understood as belonging to metaphysics what might identity mean in 'a new theoretical space where the very notion of identity is challenged?' (Kristeva 1981: 209). She makes clear however that she is not suggesting or aspiring towards a 'totality of one of the sexes and thus an effacing of difference' (p. 209). Rather she advocates:

> What I mean is, first of all, the demassification of the problematic of difference, which would imply, in a first phase, an apparent de-dramatization of the 'fight to the death' between rival groups and thus between the sexes. And this is not in the name of reconciliation – feminism has at least had the merit of showing what is irreducible and even deadly in the social contract – but in order that the struggle,

41

the implacable difference, the violence be conceived in the
very place where it operates with the maximum intransigence, in other words, in personal and sexual identity itself,
so as to make it disintegrate in its very nucleus (p. 209).

By reading Jane's play through Kristeva's three strategies
Liz was able to formulate the following conclusions. First
it is vital that Jane gains access to the male symbolic in
order to both use and subvert it. Furthermore it is also
necessary for her to elaborate on what it means to be
female in terms other than patriarchal narratives, where
femininity is reduced to an inferior way of being. However, while important, neither of these two strategies will
bring about a non-discriminatory social order. This is
because 'they can always be and are always being coun-
teracted' (Davies 1989: 71). Therefore the problems
faced in deconstructing a sexist world must ultimately be
resolved through work at the third tier where the opposition between masculinity and femininity is decon-
structed in order to challenge notions of identity.
Effectively this necessitates perceiving Jane as a subject in
process rather than an individual whose identity is fixed
in specific ways. Bronwyn Davies (1989) continues this
theme. She calls for children to have the freedom to
position themselves in multiple ways, some of which will
be recognizably 'feminine', some 'masculine' (as we currently understand these terms) and some totally unrelated to current discursive practices. What this might
imply is that on some occasions and in some instances
certain masculine and feminine characteristics might still
be worth celebrating but 'without the destructive mar-
ginalisation of the feminine and without the restrictions
currently placed on people to be exclusively or primarily
one or the other' (Davies 1989: 141). In the following
chapter we expand on what some of the repercussions are
– particularly the benefits – when research into gender is

premised on a subject who is 'fragmented' and as a consequence 'always in process'.

Note

1. Home Corners are a familiar feature within early years settings across the UK. Here various artefacts based on what would be found in typical homes are provided, including armchairs and a settee as well as facsimiles of other domestic items such as a cooking stove, plastic crockery, saucepans and so on. These items are all scaled down so that not only are they 'child-sized' they also take up considerably less room than the 'real thing'. Very often – as in Liz's classroom – children have access to dressing-up clothes in order to augment and assist further in the children's socio-dramatic play.

3

Researching Gender: A Postmodern Perspective

All fixed, fast-frozen relationships, with their train of venerable ideas and opinions, are swept away, all new-formed ones become obsolete before they can ossify. All that is solid melts into the air ... (Marx and Engels 1969: 70).

Introduction

What happens when the researcher tries to mix both feminism and postmodernism in order to untangle some of the complexities of gender? In this chapter our efforts are located around illustrating some of the repercussions when these two *isms* collide. We begin by first drawing out certain features that contribute towards defining post-modernism before moving to distinguish some of the similarities between postmodernism and feminism. We then highlight their differences. An example of Liz's research is then used where we mark out certain reper-cussions, particularly the benefits when postmodernism is brought into a study on gender.

A postmodern perspective

Perhaps we should begin by addressing the question 'What is postmodernism?' before disentangling how this effects how we see and understand our social worlds. As a first step we have to acknowledge the inadequacy of our own question because it suggests that we can offer a definitive answer. 'Postmodernism' is a very loose term that is used to describe 'the larger cultural shifts of a post-industrial, post-colonial era' (Lather 1991: 4). These shifts include economic changes (the move from mass production to flexible specialization), political changes (the collapse of the eastern European bloc and a lack of confidence in Marxism) and social changes – the so-called fragmentation of social classes as a consequence of marketing lifestyle niches. Furthermore, these upheavals when combined with the communication explosion, particularly in the visual media of film and television, work at splintering social cohesion and coherence. These are replaced by 'cultural images and social forms and identities marked by fragmentation, multiplicity, plurality and indeterminacy' (Thompson 1992: 223).

Hence the expression 'all that is solid melts into the air' both captures and characterizes the transformations that have been briefly referred to above. We can no longer have faith in or a commitment to what are termed 'overarching' or 'metanarratives' such as Marxism or other totalizing metatheories of scientific progress stemming from the Enlightenment – all of which make universalized claims. Within postmodernism such theories do not have the capacity to do 'justice to the diversity and fragmentation of postmodernity' (Thompson 1992: 225). Fraser and Nicholson (1990) in drawing upon Lyotard (1984) expand further:

> The postmodern condition is one in which 'grand narratives of legitimation' are no longer credible. By grand

45

> narratives he [Lyotard] means overarching philosophies of history like the Enlightenment story of the gradual but steady progress of reason and freedom, Hegel's dialectic of Spirit coming to know itself, and, most importantly, Marx's drama of the forward march of human productive capacities via class conflict culminating in proletarian revolution (p. 22).

Besides a loss of confidence in overarching theories postmodern thinkers also have a different conception of language. In Chapter 1 we noted how the Modernist conception of language was relatively unproblematic where there was a presupposed 'tight and identifiable relation between what was said (the signified or "message") and how it was being said (the signifier or "medium")' (Thompson 1992: 229). In contrast postmodernists perceive the '*what* was said' and '*how* it was said' as inherently unstable. In brief they argue that words gain their meaning from being part of a sequential chain within each sentence. Links can and do however break down and additionally sequences can and do become disjointed with the consequence that meaning becomes fragmented. Within this conceptualization language cannot be relied upon. That is language no longer offers certainty. Hence with a social endeavour such as research the notion that language can offer us control gets dissipated. However this does not imply that there is no such thing as meaning. Nor does it mean that the task of applying meaning should be abandoned. Instead there is recognition that any interpretations are both temporary and specific to the context or practices within which they are produced. Lather (1991) describes these processes as a 'working out'. She also opts to incorporate the term 'post-structural' when 'doing' the working out. So while postmodernism is the term she sometimes favours when discussing cultural shifts she also uses 'post-structural' to mean 'the working out of those shifts within the arenas of academic theory' (1991: 4).

Postmodernism and feminism: their similarities ... and their differences

In Chapter 2 there was an opportunity to see Liz trying to 'work out' what it means to be 'a woman'. In this chapter our focus is primarily on 'gender' and 'gender relations' where our efforts are directed at thinking about or 'working out' these issues from a postmodern perspective. Our ambition is to try to understand gender and gender relations without turning to accounts that resort to essentialist notions of what it means to be male or female – accounts that by necessity have to depend upon binary ways of thinking.

As we noted in Chapter 1 both feminism and postmodernism interrogate the inherent homocentric nature of all the fundamental dichotomies that have characterized Enlightenment reasoning and Western thinking generally, including subject/object, rational/irrational, reason/emotion and language/reality (Hekman 1990; Hallberg 1992). Embedded within these dichotomies are certain presuppositions including the notion of a coherent, unified self plus the idea of a rationalist and individual model of knowing. Effectively what both postmodernism and feminism are demanding is that the Enlightenment epistemology must be displaced and that a different way of describing human knowledge and its acquisition must be found. Now while both might be united in these demands nevertheless for feminists postmodernism poses a severe stumbling block because of its attitude towards and its treatment of 'the subject'. In general terms postmodern thinkers conceptualize the subject as 'fragmented'. Hall offers the following succinct description:

> We can no longer conceive of the individual in terms of a whole, centred, stable and completed Ego or autonomous, rational self. The 'self' is conceptualised as more fragmented and incomplete, composed of multiple selves or identities in relation to the different social world we inhabit, something with a history, produced in process. The subject is differently placed or positioned by different discourses or practices (Hall 1992: 84).

Any outright rejection of the ideals of the Enlightenment project leaves feminism in a curious and anomalous position. In Chapter 2 we identified how feminists take the concept of 'woman' as an indispensable point of reference both in terms of feminist theory and feminist politics. As Nye puts it, 'There must be a centre from which to begin weaving feminist theory, a foothold from which action can be initiated and take on meaning and strength' (Nye 1988: 4).

As a consequence, the fundamental and homocentric assumptions of the Enlightenment project have to be questioned, challenged and disputed (Alcoff 1988: 405). But on the other hand, the feminist movement is itself historically and theoretically rooted in the Enlightenment project (Hekman 1990: 2). Again in Chapter 2 we foregrounded how the first systematic justifications of women's rights were borrowed from liberal and democratic theory – movements which are derived from Modernity. But given the challenge of postmodern thinking, is it possible to have a politics of subjectivity when the subject is considered as fragmented? Can feminism incorporate post-structuralist theories given it is these that seek to dissolve and render fluid the 'self'? Is it possible in contemporary times to maintain those bits of the

Enlightenment that appear to serve feminism, including for example the emancipatory impulse of liberalism? Should feminism 'hold on to the intentions of the Enlightenment, feeble as they may be, or should we declare the whole project of modernity a lost cause ...?' (Habermas 1985: 9). Derrida introduces a possible way out of the conundrum when he declares, 'never to give up on the Enlightenment'. But as he cautions, this requires: 're-reading and re-interpreting ... to raise new questions ... disturb stereotypes and good consciences, and to complicate or rework, for a changed situation' (1994: 34).

Raising new questions

In order to provide a context in which to raise new questions we are offering some data that is again taken from Liz's research journal. Using the data we want to ask questions that circulate around 'gender relations'. We are proposing that although in this instance our questions are set against the backdrop of a nursery classroom they will nevertheless find resonance with those who while sharing our interests in gender and its performances are researching in different contexts.

The example that is offered centres on three children who at the time of writing were all aged 4 and who all attended nursery on a full-time basis. Of the three two were girls – Keeley and Jessica – while the third was a boy called Brent. The children when playing draw upon a cartoon series, *The Power Rangers*. This was a programme that was a regular feature of children's television at the time when Liz was immersed in fieldwork. *The Power Rangers* are all superheroes and as befitting the role of superhero spend considerable time and energy vanquishing evil. Interestingly at the time when the children were viewing the series two of the *Rangers* were women who were called 'Kimberley' and 'Treeny'.

An example of play

Keeley and Jessica have borrowed lengths of cloth from the dressing-up box. These are tied round their necks as capes. Both girls have their arms stretched out in front of them (a position I have come to associate with 'superhero play'). As they run they sing loudly, 'Power Rangers'. Brent, catching sight of the girls, joins them. He shapes his hands into claw-like talons and his voice – when he speaks – is deep and growly.

> Brent: *I'm coming to get you. I'm coming to catch you. I'm the monster. I'm the GREEN monster.*
> Brent intersperses his words with yells and shrieks. The girls look as if they are about to run from Brent but then Jessica stops and approaches him. Again her arms are stretched straight out in front of her.
> Jessica: *I'm Kimberley. I live in the Power Ranger story and I fight everyone.*
> As she announces her intentions to *fight everyone* she too changes her hands into talons, her tone of voice into a growl and her facial expression into a 'monster face'. Brent and Jessica face one another in what seems like a position of confrontation. Keeley then moves between the two. She still has her arms stretched out in front of her.
> Keeley: *I'm Alicia. There's no hitting and we live in the story. We're girls. We're gentle.*
> Brent: *I'm strong. I look after them. I like them. I kiss them.*
> The children run round the room, each of them holding their arms straight out and singing loudly, 'Power Rangers ... Power Rangers'.

So, what questions are prompted by this extract and in what way might they be considered as 'new'? First it has to be recognized that the issue of whether a question is new or not is irrevocably entangled with the subjectivity of the individual attempting to formulate the new question. So in watching the children Liz is no innocent bystander. Given Liz's immersion in feminism it is inevitable that this will in part influence any interpretations that she brings to the children's play. In Chapter 2 we have already noted what some of the repercussions were when a feminist framework was brought to an example of play. There was, as we saw, a tendency for Liz to wonder whether the play of Jane and her 'baby' should or should not be encouraged because of the possibility of its being 'inappropriate'. And that this 'inappropriateness' came about because the play seemed to draw from and be reliant on an essentialist notion of what it means to be 'a woman'. In similar ways she initially wondered whether Keeley, Brent and Jessica were drawn to and were using a particular narrative of 'masculinity'. Was their play being informed by an essentialist notion of what it means to be 'male'? And if it was should Liz be countenancing it or discouraging it? These were however both 'old' questions and ones moreover that polarized play so that it was either good or bad. So how do you move yourself out of this way of thinking?

An aspect of post-structuralist theory, particularly in the work associated with Jacques Derrida, is directed at practices of deconstruction. It was to Derrida that Liz moved to in order to ascertain whether she could indeed 'raise new questions' – questions moreover that might move beyond and even resist dichotomies including those relating to 'appropriate' and 'inappropriate' play.

In the main, Derrida's work centres on a sustained attack on what he considers to be the authoritarianism of Western thought and, in particular, its commitment to essentialism. A vivid example of essentialism in Western thought is the practice or phenomenon known as 'logo-centricity': the belief that words are representations of meanings already present in the speaker's mind (Sim 1996: 429). Thus speech has been conceptualized posi-tively as an index of presence, identity, unity and imme-diacy while in contrast writing can be seen as an index of absence, difference, multiplicity and distance (Kearney 1986: 119). For Derrida the relationship between speech and transparency of meaning is the heritage of logo-centrism and phonocentrism, which he explains as 'the absolute proximity of voice and being, of voice and the meaning of being, of voice and the identity of meaning' (Derrida 1976: 12). Overall, Derrida rejects the concep-tion of meaning as a fixed entity awaiting representation by either a spoken or written word. Instead he calls for:

> the joyous affirmation of the play of the world and the innocence of becoming, the affirmation of a world of signs without fault, without truth, and without origin which is offered to an active interpretation (1978: 292).

When involved in his own 'active interpretations', Derrida engages with practices of deconstruction. In decon-structing a piece of text, Derrida's objective is to reveal the ambivalences, the contradictions and the double-blinds that lie within the text, and he does this by disturbing the binary structuring around which the text is organized. As Derrida highlights, binaries are not peaceful partnerships but function as a consequence of domination:

> We are not dealing with a peaceful co-existence of a vis-à-vis, but rather with a violent hierarchy. One of the terms gov-erns the other (axiologically, logically, etc.), or has the upper hand, occupies the commanding position. To

deconstruct the opposition, first of all, is to overturn the hierarchy at a given moment (1981: 41).

It is important to note, however, that the aim is not simply to reverse polarities – this would just be another instance of structure, where 'the hierarchy of dual oppositions always establishes itself' (Derrida 1981: 42). Rather, the aim of deconstruction is to 'keep the process from degrading into structure' (Cooper 1989: 483). Derrida does this by foregrounding how there is a constant double movement within the opposition so that the positively valued term is defined only by contrast to the negatively valued term which continually threatens the former's sovereignty (Cooper 1989: 483).

Engaging with deconstruction entails involving one of Derrida's most important concepts, that of *différence*. Derrida capitalizes on the wordplay that circulates around *différence*, combining as it does two French words with a similar sound quality (*différence* and *différance*, 'difference' and 'deferral' respectively). It seems that, for Derrida, *différence* is to be understood as a continuous movement, something which is always just out of reach and, as a consequence, never fully present. What logocentrism attempts is to delay or defer this movement of difference so that a philosophy of presence can be maintained. Thus we can go on believing in and colluding with the notion 'that things and events are given to us as fully constituted experiences' (Cooper 1989: 489).

Deconstructing the children's story

Above we have already hinted at some of the reasons why the children's play might be causing Liz some discomfort. In brief, all 'superhero' stories are premised on and underpinned by a 'goody/baddy' narrative structure.

That is, 'baddies' whether they are people, monsters or aliens, are set upon committing some wickedness against the world but are prevented from doing so by 'goodies'. It is this narrative that informs the *Power Ranger* cartoon series which in turn has informed the children's play. However, both in the cartoon series and indeed in the children's play the narrative includes women. So it could be argued that the inclusion of women as 'superheroes' is a step in the right direction towards equity between the sexes. However, the legitimating discursive practices that the programme privileges are uniformly male, where, for example, men are strong and active, while women are passive and weak. So, the inclusion of women in the story is done on the basis of the women becoming 'token' males. The hierarchy between the male/female couplet has not been tampered with; rather, it has been reinforced.

What about the children's interpretation of the *Power Rangers* story? What are the binaries that structure their story, and as a consequence, what polarizations are implied? It would seem that the two girls position themselves at either end of a polarization. Thus, at one end of the spectrum is Jessica's 'Kimberley' whose character valorizes certain attributes, including fighting. So while her name denotes her as female, she is a fighter, a trait that within the superhero genre is associated with the male. As a consequence Jessica's 'Kimberley' does not pose any threat or challenge to the consistent male/female coupling where the male is always the positive. So, within the confines of the children's story, Jessica too is a token male.

In sharp contrast, Keeley offers us the character of 'Alicia'. As 'Alicia' Keeley seems to epitomize all that is traditionally considered as 'feminine'. For example, it may be recalled that she refutes hitting – *I'm Alicia. There's no hitting* and furthermore she stresses that *We're girls.*

We're gentle thereby implying a relationship between gender and specific forms of behaviour. Interestingly, in the series that the children would have been watching there was not a female character called 'Alicia'. There was however a 'Treeny', a name that in Keeley's terms might have lacked a certain feminine grace.

What about Brent and his play? In what way would this perturb Liz? Initially Liz felt that Brent's character was drawn from and attached to a hegemonic account of masculinity. When he appears as the 'green monster' he seemed to her to represent the 'bad forces' that in narratives such as superhero tales come to get the innocent and the good. His voice, hands and face were in her view used to emphasize his 'badness'. However when challenged he exchanges this character and assumes another guise. He states: *I'm strong. I look after them. I like them. I kiss them.* As such there seemed to be an implication that because he was the strong male he then had to assume responsibilities such as 'looking after' the girls. Indeed he also gets to kiss them. In Liz's eyes Brent's position at the end of the story was similar to that of the prince featured in numerous fairy stories, who, having slain the monster/ dragon, then brings the tale to some kind of resolution with a magical kiss. As Davies (1989) points out, a key element in this particular construction of masculinity is the 'fact' that 'the idea of what it is to be male is constructed in opposition to the *idea* of femaleness' (ibid: 89, original emphasis). In effect, what this means is that when the boys are acting out stories which are informed by the 'goody/baddy' narrative, they 'must in part position themselves as masculine through oppressive acts of domination and control of their environment and non-masculine others' (ibid). Given this analysis Liz was led to consider that the children, via their assumed guises and within the confines of specific binaries which structure the narrative, had invested in subjectivities that are quintessentially essentialist in nature. That is, the play of the children, while on the one hand make-believe – a fantasy – is nevertheless supported by a supposed 'truth' about what it means to be 'male' and 'female'. Again Liz found herself vexed with repetitive worries. How could she, for example, as the teacher, prevent herself and the children in her care from locating individuals and themselves in categories that rest upon and are supported by the powerful/subordinate nexus? Were there any possibilities for encouraging the boys to act out stories that incorporated other forms of masculinity?

Judith Butler's (1990) work assisted Liz in her rethinking. Butler refutes the idea of one's subjectivity as stemming from some inner core. Interestingly she sees both genders in terms of them being an act that is put on, where the things we wear and the actions we make all conspire to give our gender identities substance. Being 'male' or being 'female' is within her terms a charade or an illusion that is 'discursively maintained for the purpose of the regulation of sexuality within the obligatory frame of reproductive heterosexuality' (Butler 1990: 37). In deconstructing *the* boy and *the* girl Butler disturbs psychoanalytical theory where the existence of a primary identification or primary repression 'instantiates gender specificity and subsequently informs, organizes, and unifies identity' (ibid: 329). She elaborates further:

> By grounding the metanarratives in a myth of origin, the psychoanalytical description of gender identity confers a false sense of legitimacy and universality to a culturally specific and, in some contexts, culturally oppressive version of gender identity (ibid: 330).

In destabilizing psychoanalytical theory Butler urges us to consider variations so that gender identity is considered in more provisional ways. Effectively the girls when dressed as *Power Rangers* are parodying maleness but we should not assume that there is an original 'which such parodic identities imitate' (ibid: 338).

Butler's theoretical framing with its emphasis on performance made Liz much more conscious of the way the children played with categorizations. For instance the girls' capes plus their outstretched arms marked them out as superheroes. It would have been these trappings that would have relayed particular signals to Brent. Having received them they then informed his response. Given his particular reaction where he metamorphosed himself into a fierce green monster it is understandable that Jessica rejoined with a more or less similar characterization. Her creation 'Kimberley' was equally as fierce and it looked for a time as if the only option in terms of story development was for the two children to fight. However because of the way Keeley portrayed her character 'Alicia' she was able to achieve several things. First, she managed to destabilize what is effectively a repetitive storyline because she prevented the two protagonists, Brent and Jessica, from having to battle it out. True she had to resort to coupling *girls* with *gentleness*. But in a sense what other characterizations does she have available to her within the story? If she is to make sense to both her companions while at the same time affecting some kind of dramatic transition so that a fight does not occur, her parody has to practise Derrida's double-blind so as to 'overturn the hierarchy at a given moment' (Derrida 1981: 41). Keeley's characterization of *Alicia* skitters from one performance to another where anatomically she is a girl but by cross-dressing, which in this instance meant donning a cape and putting her arms out straight, she becomes a boy. It is this performance of a boy that is challenged by Brent. As a consequence she overlays her boy character with a female performance. She performs as a drag queen where the signifiers of both *girl* and *gentleness* disarm and seduce

57

both her companions into compliance so that a fight does not break out. And what of Brent's final line:

I'm strong. I look after them. I like them. I kiss them.?

It would seem from the analysis that has been rehearsed above that Liz's preliminary thoughts had been to categorize Brent's play within a stereotypical account of what constitutes a male where she had understood his mannerisms and other acts as being indicative of a male and one moreover who was acting in predatory ways. So his declaration of *I'm strong* was for her tied to the notion of the tough male whose toughness is drawn from and is premised on the weak female. But Brent adds other trappings to his idea of 'strong'. He appends the notions of both 'looking after' and 'liking' girls as well. We could say that Brent – just as Keeley did – undertakes certain transformations so that the green monster is submerged by characterizations which are habitually seen as feminine and which are very often negatively construed. Again perhaps what we are witnessing within Brent's portrayal is his capacity to 'keep the process from degrading into structure' (Cooper 1989: 483) while having to maintain the structure of the story so that it makes sense to all three players.

Conclusion

As we remarked at the beginning of this chapter both feminism and postmodernism have 'elaborated deep reaching criticisms of the institution of philosophy' (Fraser and Nicholson 1990: 19). But, and this is a significant *but*, a gap does reside between the two. Fraser and Nicholson describe this divide in the following way:

Postmodernists have focused primarily on the philosophy side of the problem. They have begun by elaborating anti-foundational metaphilosophical perspectives and from these have drawn conclusions about the shape and character of social criticism. For feminists, on the other hand, the question of philosophy has always been subordinate to an interest in social criticism. Consequently, they have begun by developing critical political perspectives and from there have drawn conclusions about the status of philosophy ... each of the two perspectives suggests some important criticisms of the other. A postmodern reflection on feminist theory reveals disabling vestiges of essentialism whilst a feminist reflection on postmodernism reveals androcentrism and political naiveté (pp. 19–20).

We would suggest that Liz has used the play as if it were an allegory, and in her treatment of the allegory she has drawn upon both postmodernism and on feminism. Thus, she began by responding to its surface meaning. As we have seen it was her feminist self that framed her initial interpretations and the desire to do this stemmed from those 'social criticisms' she holds in relation to contemporary gender relations. As with all allegories, the characters, the plot and other symbolism that lie within it act as conduits and ciphers for certain truths and morality. In the children's story it was to the underpinning 'truths' concerned with what it means to be 'male' and 'female' and additionally certain codes of behaviour and relations of power which circulated between the two sexes that Liz directed post-structuralist theories. In so doing she was able to follow Derrida's advice so as to re-read and reinterpret the children's play. Simply to offer a feminist reading would, we think, probably have necessitated Liz reinstating a series of binaries where as an example the play would have been categorized into types such as 'appropriate' and 'inappropriate' and the children's actions would have been read against some essentialist idea of what it means to be a 'girl' and a 'boy'. Having troubled some of the 'foundations' that underpinned the play of the children, Liz's subsequent actions within her classroom were driven by feminist desires and aspirations. In trying to get to grips with the children's play it did seem to Liz that the three children were themselves active in trying to broaden those meanings that are brought to the category of 'boy' and 'girl'. Both within the classroom and outside in the wider world the children are in a continuous struggle to understand who they are. They are constantly learning, accommodating and, at times, rejecting those discourses that work at shaping identities. What were Liz's responsibilities within this process? What role could she play so as to assist the children to resist or redefine powerful discursive practices? Could she assist them to use their own resources so as to mobilize discursive practices in order to develop more equitable relations? What seemed apparent to Liz was that within the children's play they were themselves capable of agency. Each of them could and did utilize the knowledge – power nexus so as to act and to act confidently. How could Liz develop this capacity further?

What became plain to Liz in the course of her research was that in order to assist the children she had to attend to her own disposition to read, understand and categorize the world in particular ways. By engaging with postmodernism and with feminism Liz became ever mindful of 'one's present status and condition so that one might see it more intensely, and to know one's circumstances deeply in order to recognise recurring games of truth' (Pignatelli 1993: 418).

We have come to see the children's play plus Liz's interpretations of it as acts of deconstruction where children and teacher alike have tried to be sceptical of received wisdom about gender and gender relations. For Liz what became noticeable to her as she went about her business of being a nursery teacher was that by engaging with both feminism and postmodernism she moved from saying 'Is it true?' to 'Who wants it to be true? What are the effects of saying this is true and not that?' As Pignatelli notes, 'Asking such questions forces teachers to recognise that they are not only critically engaged with, but also constituted within, these [truth] regimes' (ibid: 421).

Note

A version of this chapter first appeared as a Colloquium in the journal *Contemporary Issues in Early Childhood* (2002) 3 (1), 139–46). We are grateful to the editors for permission to reproduce it here.

4

Researching Gender: Issues of Masculinity

Introduction

This chapter explores the ways in which some researchers and commentators have perceived feminism as undermining what it means to be male and as affecting adversely the performance of boys in a school system that has become more concerned about girls. If feminism tends to be associated with the left and with a postmodern view of the creation of gender identities, the new masculinism tends to be associated with the right and with biological determinism (see, for example, Apple 2001). The new masculinism appeals to what are perceived to be 'common-sense' biologically based differences between male and female (see Lingard and Douglas 1999). It is based in a form of essentialism that sees identity as immutable in terms not only of gender but of social class and ethnicity. However, drawing on his research, Ian explores the ways in which such views oversimplify all forms of identity and seeks to explore the potential and the challenges of moving towards non-hegemonic identities.

Disadvantaged girls?

Educational gender-related research in the 1970s and 1980s was primarily concerned with the inequalities experienced by girls. Younger *et al.* (2005) identify a number of themes in this research. One (Sharpe 1976; Deem 1980) explored the ways in which subject choice at secondary level was premised on stereotypical notions of the qualifications needed for particular gendered careers. Another theme centred on the ways in which boys dominated classrooms, receiving more teacher attention (see e.g., Mahony 1985). A connected concern (Myers 2000), as research and practice began to examine ways of increasing girls' confidence and attainment in subjects where these had previously lagged behind those of boys, explored the ways in which boys limited girls' opportunities when carrying out practical work in mathematics, science and technology.

Underachieving boys?

The 1990s, however, began to see growing concern about the educational achievements of boys (Warrington and Younger 2000). On the one hand, evidence from public examinations and from assessments at the ages of 7, 11 and 14 was indicating that boys were not achieving as highly or progressing as rapidly as girls. On the other, there was growing attention to the disaffection of boys with school, with attendant issues in relation to behaviour and attendance. This 'underperformance' has been explained in a number of ways. Archer and Yamashita (2003: 116) point to 'the challenges to rationality and rise of feminism' and Younger *et al.* (2005) to the crisis for masculinity caused by male unemployment. Within the popular press, there has been particular interest in explanations which focus on claims for biological, hormonal and brain differences between boys and girls (Biddulph 1998; Hoff Sommers 2000; Gurian and Henley 2001; Archer and Lloyd 2002, Baron-Cohen 2003) and a concern that these different needs are not being met because schools have become focused on girls. This is often seen as further exacerbated in primary schools by an increasingly female workforce. As fewer men have chosen to train and to work as teachers this is seen as creating feminized learning environments ill-suited to the perceived needs of boys. As Martino and Berrill (2003) and Younger *et al.* (2005) identify, there has been panic over the supposed plight of boys as the 'new masculinism' has sought to reclaim the educational landscape from its supposed preoccupation with meeting the needs of girls.

Alongside these essentialist explanations of the reasons for differences in attainment between boys and girls, other explanations have focused on how constructs of masculinity can come to cause conflict with school expectations. Connell (1989) explores the ways in which, while some working-class boys see the economic value of success and so find ways of being male that are focused on educational achievement, the responses of other working-class boys to the authority of the educational system are negative and lead them into a counter-culture where educational success is highly undesirable. What begins to emerge from further research is the importance of a more nuanced approach to understanding the differences in attainment. Younger *et al.* (2005) and Martino and Berrill (2003) have drawn attention to the importance of understanding that not all boys do badly and that not all girls do well. Gorrard *et al.* (1999, 2001) have examined the ways in which a more detailed analysis of examination and assessment results does not support a universal trend of girls doing better than boys: there are different trends at different ages and in different subjects and socio-economic circumstances appear to be particularly significant for both boys and girls in terms of achievement.

Another common theme in the literature (Mac an Ghaill 1994; Jordan 1995; Skelton 1996; Jackson 2003; Swain 2004) is the way in which boys of different ages 'do masculinity'. With younger children this is concerned with behaviours such as play fighting. As boys get older, it involves performances that indicate toughness and athleticism. In the secondary school years, in addition, boys become concerned with demonstrating apparently effortless success and with normative notions of sexuality. These ways of acting maleness can be perceived as being aimed at marking out difference from the necessary Other: the female. A notion of gender as performance emerges (see, for example, Paechter 1998, 2003a, 2003b, 2006; Butler 1999, 2004) and, more than that, there is an examination of the importance of recognizing that there is not one performance but many. What also emerges is a sense in which gender is not fixed but fluid and cannot be separated from other forms of identity such as ethnicity, race, religion and class (see e.g., Brah 1996; Archer and Yamashita 2003) and a further sense in which, despite this fluidity, moving beyond the fixings is difficult because of the ways in which, following Foucault (1998, 2002), power operates to suggest that some identities are more acceptable and more worthwhile than others, causing problems in constructing and negotiating gender identities that do not conform to the binary division. The work of Renold (2004), for example, explores the difficulties that boys of primary school age experienced in her research when they attempted to move away from hegemonic forms of masculinity.

Loosening the fixings?

Ian's experiences of working in a nursery school where different ethnic and religious groups came together led to an interest in carrying out research that explored what ethnic, religious, gender and class identities mean in such a context, how they relate to each other and how they come to affect children's experiences of early schooling. The nursery is one where Ian was the head teacher ten years previously and where the intake is made up of approximately four-fifths children of Pakistani heritage, the majority of whom speak Punjabi at home, and one-fifth children of white indigenous origin, who speak English at home. Despite Ian's awareness of literature that has challenged the hegemony of the supposed lessons of developmental psychology (see e.g., Burman 1994, 1999; Morss 1996; James 1999; Jeffcoate, cited in Short 1999) and drawn attention to the way in which understandings about children and childhood are, in large part, social and cultural constructs, Ian started out on the process interested to study how children's ethnic identity 'developed' during the nursery years. In retrospect, this reflected the scientific rationalism (and maleness?) inherent in the way in which developmental psychology has been particularly influential in the field of early childhood education and has traditionally understood identity as stable and unfolding from within according to a predetermined and normative pattern. Piaget (1954) and followers such as Schaffer (1996) have considered that understandings of social categories, such as those relating to ethnic identity, form relatively late because they are seen as requiring understandings about self and other, whole and part, that are not possible until middle childhood. Further influences on understandings about identity in early childhood have come from psychoanalytical approaches, such as Freud's psychosexual theory (1991), which have been concerned with how the individual's identity is formed through a process of sexuality and gender identification, first with the parents and then with the wider world. There is little consideration, however, of other aspects of identity, such as ethnicity, and gender and sexuality are seen as fixed and stable and the drive is towards an essentialist and normative notion of what being male and female means and towards the supposed ideal of heterosexuality.

All this suggests a model of the world that sees identity as fixed and stable and life as a journey towards logical truths and facts that can be discovered. Ian was dissatisfied with these accounts, however, and interested in seeking to understand children's identities in ways other than the dominant discourses of developmental psychology. It proved challenging to move towards understanding identity in ways that broke free of construction purely within the individual. More recent accounts were explored, such as those by Lacan (1989) and Henriques *et al.* (1998) but, while in many ways they reflect a poststructuralist position, they also retain many psychoanalytical pre-given notions. The emphasis on the notion of the Phallus, for example, as the 'necessary other' in such accounts of identity work creates a theoretical model underpinned by a binary that is formed by contrast with the masculine. This together with the concern with internal psychosexual conflicts is suggestive of essentialist notions of gender and sexuality. The work of Sondergaard (2002) and Boldt (2002) was considered helpful in challenging internal models of understanding aspects of identity. Sondergaard (ibid: 452) argues that 'we do not require constructs such as needs, repressions and psychosexual conflicts' and suggests that what is needed is an understanding of the ways in which the 'discursive repertoires' (ibid) that occur in local contexts construct aspects of identity such as gender, sexuality and ethnicity and of the ways in which these reflect context-specific as well as sociocultural and historical understandings. Such a conceptualization begins to fuse the cognitive with the social in a constant interplay of negotiated and distributed iterative practices spanning the individual and the communities in which s/he lives. In place of a view of identity as an internally driven process, they suggest that what is then needed is an understanding of how these aspects of identity become incorporated into individual consciousness through a process of sifting and synthesizing.

While this literature is useful in exploring gender and sexual aspects of children's identities, the interest in considering the interplay with ethnicity meant that it was important to examine more specifically research concerned with children's ethnic identity. However, while there are numerous studies of ethnic identity and schooling in adolescence (e.g. Phinney 1990, 1996; Bhatti 1999) and a smaller number concerned with the primary years (e.g. Connolly 1995, 1998; Brooker 2002), there are very few indeed, in English, that consider the nursery years. Classic developmental psychology studies of ethnicity in schools, such as those by Aboud (1988) and Finkelstein and Haskins (1983) (and others by, e.g., Adler 2001; Kowalski and Lo 2001; Kowalski 2003) were not considered helpful because they are concerned with developmental stage-based models of ethnic identity and with ethnic and racial colour difference understood in cognitive terms and reflect an essentialist view of ethnic identity.

There is, however, a growing interest in postmodern and social constructivist approaches to ethnic identity and young children, emerging, in the West, from a group of Australian and some American academics who are interested particularly in equity programmes (see e.g., Yelland 1998, 2005; MacNaughton 2000, 2003; Grieshaber and

Cannella 2001; Rhedding-Jones 2001; Cannella and Viruru 2004). However, as Skattebol (2005: 189) notes 'there
is a lack of critical theory around ways that children are
positioned through ethnicity and gender' (and, Ian
would argue, following Dwyer (2000), how the researchers themselves adopt positions). It is also the case that
while work on gender from this tradition is underpinned
by post-structuralism, the tendency is to view ethnic
identity in ways that suggest essentialism. Rhedding-Jones
(2002: 94) argues that 'moving towards fluid multi-
plicities, where people belong to a range of simultaneously operating categories, beyond a binary, remains a
challenge' and explains this in terms of arguing that 'a
shifting ethnicity in post-modernity includes the modernist fixing of identity, as related to race, religion, country
of residence and change' (Rhedding-Jones 2001: 152).

Fixing matters

Despite this conviction that understandings were needed
that went beyond the dominant binaries, some aspects of
Ian's research appeared, initially, to reinforce fixings in
relation to identity. The research began with visits to the
children's homes in the summer before they started
attending the nursery school. This was intended to enable
Ian to understand something of the children's homes and
prior experiences and to consider how these might
influence the children's responses as they started nursery
school. In most of the homes of the children of Pakistani
heritage, religion was a significant element in what the
children experienced at home. In only one of the homes
of the white children was religion a significant factor. In
this home, there were nine Bibles on the bookcases,
crosses on the doors and a t-shirt that said 'Jesus Loves
Me' hanging on a radiator. Most of the homes of families

of Pakistani heritage were filled with framed extracts from the Qur'ān and ornaments and pictures of mosques. In one of the homes, a grandmother prayed during our visit and in another there was a radio receiver on the wall with prayers being broadcast from the local mosque. Where there was a strong influence from Islam and where Punjabi was the language mostly spoken at home, the children were hesitant towards the nursery staff and towards Ian as the researcher during the visits. Predictably, these were also the children who were most upset when they arrived at nursery. While they did seek contact with the staff, they were often reluctant to play with any of the equipment or materials.

The nursery environment in which the children found themselves appeared to function as a border marker that elicited a variety of responses. All the children could be seen to face significant differences in the scale and size of the nursery school and its open-plan nature in comparison with their relatively small, predominantly terraced homes. The types of activities offered were reasonably characteristic of what the wealthier white children may have experienced at home but were probably less familiar for the other children. The 'white' homes had relatively few signs of print in relation to what was seen in the poorest Muslim homes because of the significant number of texts from the Qur'ān. This led to the white children experiencing a great deal more text at nursery than at home and the children of Pakistani heritage seeing a great deal less, and what there was did not reflect the Arabic and Urdu found in their homes. The Home Corner was reasonably representative of the very small number of wealthier white homes but had little in common with the homes of the less affluent white children and with many of the homes of the children of Pakistani heritage. This seemed to lead to some of the children settling readily into a nursery environment that was relatively familiar to them, while others appeared not to know how to engage with the environment in which they found themselves. While most white children played with the nursery equipment readily enough, a minority of children of Pakistani heritage stood on the fringes. Some of these children observed for a number of days and weeks and eventually joined in but a few took almost a year to begin to engage in the nursery's activities.

On a very small number of occasions the children voiced their own views about culture and identity in ways that were strongly suggestive of essentialism. During one story time, for example, when Eid was being discussed by a white female member of staff, the children of Pakistani heritage talked about their mothers putting mendhi patterns on to their hands as part of the celebrations. One girl, however, suddenly called out that the member of staff should not decorate her hands because mendhi should not be worn by a 'white woman', suggesting that she appeared to see skin colour as a sign of what is permissible and acceptable in relation to religious and cultural practices.

In terms of friendship groupings, Ian's observations of the children seemed to indicate further evidence of fixities of gender and ethnic identity as the children played largely in same-sex, same-race groupings. Questions could be raised about whether these fixings were based on the kinship that could be held to emerge from culture, race, gender, language and common life experiences. Where there was contact between ethnic groups, this was usually in the sandpit, the construction area, the Home Corner and role-play areas and the climbing area. This might suggest that interaction was easier where action rather than language was the basis of the play. There were, however, gender differences in who played in which area too and there was a strong suggestion of gender stereotyping in terms of the activities that the children seemed to choose:

71

many more boys than girls played in the sandpit and construction areas; more girls than boys played in the Home Corner; while both boys and girls seemed to play in equal numbers in the climbing area. There were also differences in the amount of interaction that occurred that seemed to point to gender and ethnicity operating in articulation with each other. The white children were more likely to interact with each other than those of Pakistani heritage and girls of Pakistani heritage were more likely to interact than boys of Pakistani heritage.

That ethnic and gender identities appeared as factors which affected children's transition to nursery school could suggest fixity and essentialism in terms of identity. It is important to be mindful of Butler's insight (1999) that practices are 'written on the skin' but her further contention (2004) that performances becoming interiorized as beliefs is not what matters; what does is understanding how power operates to determine what is interiorized. This begins to point to the operation of power in the choices that are made. Foucault (1998, 2002) enables us to understand some of the ways in which discourses of power operate and would maintain that understandings and performances in relation to ethnic, gender, culture and class identities are underpinned by such discourses. For Foucault (2002: 340) power

> operates on the field of possibilities in which the behaviour of active subjects is able to inscribe itself. It is a set of actions on possible actions; it incites, it induces, it seduces, it makes easier or more difficult; it releases or contrives, makes more probable or less; in the extreme, it constrains or forbids absolutely ...

Moreover, performances and understandings in relation to ethnicity, gender, culture and class are not only constructed through what is done or what is said but also through what is not done and not said:

> There is no binary division to be made between what one says and what one does not say ... There is not one but many silences, and they are an integral part of the strategies that underlie and permeate discourses (1998: 27).

Discourses of power could be seen to be operating to engage white indigenous, more affluent children but to marginalize and exclude poorer white children and those of Pakistani heritage. Some of the silences in the nursery could be seen to emerge from an environment that did not reflect the worlds from which many of the children came.

The complexities of identity

In order to understand a little more of how identities are performed and experienced one needs constantly to be aware of the tendency towards binary and essentialist ways of understanding, the powerful legacy of Enlightenment ways of seeing and to seek to challenge these tendencies by 'reading against the grain' (Clarke 2005: 78). Thus, the differences between boys and girls of Pakistani heritage also began to suggest ways in which identity is more complex and multi-nodal than it might at first appear and also to support the evidence highlighted earlier in the chapter of complexity in the way that gender, class and ethnicity appear to interact in relation to attainment. While, as noted above, the influence from Islam was strong in many of the homes, it was strongest in the poor homes, where the dominant language was Punjabi, and weakest in the most wealthy, where the dominant language was English, suggesting the ways in which economic circumstances, religion and language interact as aspects of cultural and ethnic identity. The complexity of these identities was particularly evident in the house, described earlier, with a radio receiver on the wall with prayers being broadcast from the local mosque but where there was also a clock on the wall, that, while decorated with Arabic script, played 'There's no place like home'. This begins to point to the ways in which, in this community, identities of home and family were multiple, with Islam one influence alongside others. The children's attendance at local schools led them and their families into contact with the dominant, largely white culture. In the case of the particular nursery school, they entered a setting where most of the children were of Pakistani heritage but where most of the staff were white and where those of Pakistani heritage were in some of the least powerful positions.

The research also involved Ian attending meetings between staff and parents where discussions focused on how their children had settled into nursery school, and these pointed further to the complexities of understanding identity. In the case of the white family for whom religion appeared important during the home visit, other aspects of identity became significant during the parent interviews. Mitchell's father talked of taking him to the circus and Mitchell being mesmerized by a female trapeze artist who, he said, was very attractive. His father recalled how at the curtain call, Mitchell said 'Wow' when the trapeze artist stood in front of him and then asked 'If mum keeps going to keep fit, will she look like that?' This emphasis on gender and sexual identity could be considered consistent with the claims of Freud (1991) and Lacan (1989). The sense of sexual attraction that the father seemed to suggest his son felt for the trapeze artist may point to a concern on the part of the father to demonstrate that his son was developing as a heterosexual male. The comments could also be seen to point to Boldt's (2002) suggestion that such aspects of identity emerge from the narratives that are developed between parents and children rather than from the internal drives argued for in Freud's psychosexual theory (1991).

Other identities were also important for Mitchell, however, and on some occasions there were signs of binary fixings. These fixings, however, emerge from different aspects of his identity and need to be considered in relation to each other. When Ian returned to the nursery during preparations for Eid, Mitchell was making an Eid card. As Ian talked to him, he said that he would not be celebrating Eid at his house and, when asked why not, he said, 'We'll be having Christmas, silly, but not just yet'. When asked why he would not be having Eid, he replied 'Because we're not dark, are we?' He said, however, that he would like to celebrate Eid because he could get a Spiderman suit for his new clothes. He appeared to see religious events in terms of binary alternatives and to associate religious events with skin colour. He was aware that he was being brought up in a Christian household and that he was 'not dark', suggesting a construction of ethnicity and religion based on colour difference. There is also evidence of identity based on age and personal advantage, however, as religion is swept aside as a concern at the prospect of a Spiderman outfit. Religion did reappear as a significant aspect of identity towards the end of the school year, when Ian accompanied the children on a trip to the seaside. Mitchell began to talk on the train about his older brother who he said had died the previous weekend after falling downstairs. He went on to say, 'But it's not God's fault. He got drunk and fell downstairs. That's why he died – it's not God's fault'. Traditional accounts of moral development (Kohlberg 1984) would point to such understandings emerging from within but Boldt's notion (2002) of the internalization of conversations (between Mitchell and his parents, perhaps, in this case) as discursive repertoires again appears helpful in understanding his comments. Alongside a sense of fluidity in Mitchell's identities there is a sense of binaries being significant and there are serious questions about the responsibility of the nursery and the researcher in responding to and troubling the discursive repertoires that are being internalized.

This sense of fluidity and fixing was also apparent in conversations with children of Pakistani heritage. One girl, for example, commented while making her Eid card that: 'Eid isn't my happy birthday, I had my happy birthday yesterday … '. It could be suggested that she demonstrated confusion over different forms of celebration but it could also point to a concern to make sure that the personal celebration of her birthday was recognized as well as the group celebration of Eid, perhaps illustrating the ways in which children position themselves in relation to particular cultural events and practices and how different aspects of their identities are important to them in different situations.

Boundaries and identities

Identities may thus usefully be conceived of as shifting performances of the moment and bring to mind Butler's work (1999) on gender identity with its conceptualization of identity as:

> tenuously constituted in time, instituted in an exterior space through a *stylized repetition of acts* … If gender is instituted through acts which are internally discontinuous, then the *appearance of substance* is precisely that, a constructed identity, a performative accomplishment which the

social audience, including the actors themselves, come to believe and to perform in the mode of belief (p. 179).

In these performances, identities of gender, age, class, ethnicity, culture and religion are not viewed as essences but as aspects which are more or less important in relation to boundaries that mark out what is significant for children and adults in different situations. Barth (1966) sees ethnic identity as being generated through interaction with others. It relies in part on how we see ourselves but also, crucially, on how others see us in any given situation. Barth's claim is that ethnic identity is a performance in relation to a boundary but that boundary is permeable and plastic rather than fixed:

> we can assume no simple one-to-one relationship between ethnic units and cultural similarities and differences. The features that are taken into account are not the sum of 'objective' differences, but only those which the actors themselves regard as significant ... Some cultural features are used by actors as signals and emblems of differences, others are ignored ... (Barth 1969: 14).

This negotiation of identities around shifting and malleable boundaries is conceptualized by Brah (1996: 242–3) as occurring in 'diaspora spaces' where:

> individuals and collectivities are simultaneously positioned in social relations constituted and performed across multiple dimensions of differentiation; ... these categories always operate in articulation ... Power is exercised in/ through/by human discursively constituted subjects, and such operations of power are the very basis of agency.

As Brah (ibid: 67) also argues, it is important to understand 'how gender relations are constituted in articulation with class, racism, ethnicity and sexuality in the construction of ... social relations, and what types of identities are inscribed in the process'.

The diaspora spaces of identities

Diaspora spaces can be conceived of as involving multi-modal dances in relation to identity. In such spaces the allocation of meanings in relation to gender, ethnic, cultural and class differences is understood as circumstantial. Meanings are negotiated and renegotiated and are concerned with *différance* in Derrida's sense (2002) of both difference and deferral. It may be, however, as Brah (1996) argues, that such processes are possible only because essentialist definitions do exist which permit the space to develop new understandings whose final meanings are forever deferred. This notion of diaspora spaces is at the heart of how performances in relation to identity are conceived and at the very heart of the way in which research is understood (see Chapter 6). Ian's research points to a conception of identity as multiple, a network of performances that encompasses ethnicity, gender, sexuality, class and age. Once we move beyond the world as conceived in terms of binary opposites and 'one-way streets' a space opens to understand identities as shifting, ebbing and flowing in different situations that allow different forms of understanding to emerge. Instead of a view of identity as fixed from birth, there is a sense of ever-shifting and competing identities with different religious, cultural, political, economic, educational and psychological discourses having a bearing on the way in which identities are enacted in the nursery school and the children's homes.

The chapter began with discussions regarding gender, attainment and opportunities and Ian's research suggests that to point to essentialist notions of gender as the sole source of current concerns in relation to boys and schooling seems to oversimplify the complexity of the factors and identities at work. It is useful to be mindful of Bhaskar's contention (1998a) that there is no one-to-one relationship between effects, causes and structures and there may be numerous effects with numerous causes. Causes are viewed by Bhaskar (1998a) as tendencies rather than as certainties and their effects may not be seen or even actually occur. In Ian's research, there is a sense in which children are in some ways positioned but also of the ways that they find to position themselves and, moving beyond Bhaskar's notion of tendencies (1998a), identity may be understood in terms of the rhizomatic relationships introduced by Liz earlier. Thus identity is conceptualized as a rhizomatic 'journey among intersections, nodes, and regionalizations through a multi-centred complexity' (Lather 1993: 680, after Deleuze 1992: 163–4, cited in Brown and Jones 2001: 180).

Ian's research has begun to suggest some of the ways in which identity can be understood in postmodern and non-hegemonic ways. The chapter that follows will explore further the ways in which the research process itself involves 'a disregard for prescribed order and patterned ways of being' (Jones *et al.* 2005: 205).

5

Undertaking Research in a Field that is Feminized

Introduction

More detailed attention is paid in this chapter to the ways in which gender and other forms of identity are shaped and reshaped in the reflexive negotiation and interactions that form part of a particular research setting. Ian explores his own experiences of carrying out research in the feminized setting of a nursery school. He examines how far he is able to become part of particular communities of practice in relation to how gender, religion, ethnicity and class are experienced and enacted. Ian explores the ways in which he is positioned and positions himself as he feels himself variously included, excluded, elevated to expert and relegated to fool as he weaves a path among the nursery's communities of practice.

Moving beyond binaries and essentialism

As we saw in the previous chapter, the theoretical framework underpinning notions of identity changed dramatically and rapidly as Ian's ethnographic investigations began to suggest a quite different model in relation to identity from that originally conceived. Ian came to feel that identity was not located in the individual, as so often suggested by the dominant discourse of developmental psychology, but, instead, identity could be better thought of as multiple and shifting and played out between the children, the staff and Ian as the researcher. He came to feel, like Giddens (1991: 3), that 'the self, like the broader institutional contexts in which it exists, has to be reflexively made. Yet this task has to be accomplished amid a puzzling diversity of options and possibilities'.

The task in Ian's research was to explore how identities were negotiated and experienced in the practices that were enacted within a particular nursery school. Lave and Wenger's communities of practice theory (1991) was considered useful in seeking to theorize this process. Lave and Wenger's research with apprentice tailors explored the ways in which the latter initially engaged in legitimate peripheral participation in the community of practice of tailors, undertaking non-crucial tasks, which would not put the whole undertaking at risk if not completed wholly successfully, progressing to full participation. One reading of the purpose of nursery education (and indeed all education) would be that it operates in a similar way.

Significantly for the current discussion, Wenger (1998) also draws parallels between the processes that are involved in learning skills through legitimate peripheral participation in community practices and those that are involved in shaping identity. Ian began to explore ways in which the shaping of identities (those of the children, staff and Ian as researcher) were being played out in the various communities of practice in and around the nursery school. Wenger (1998) conceives of identity as being shaped in practices within localized communities but going beyond them because of the ways in which local communities relate to what Bronfenbrenner (1979) would term the macro level, involving national, cultural and societal institutions, structures and influences. This involvement in practice includes possibilities of participation and non-participation, negotiation and reification

81

of identity, and a conception of identity as a 'learning trajectory' (Wenger 1998: 149) that makes links across time and place between different communities of practice. The practice and performance of identity also involves identification with particular communities of practice, the ways in which the boundaries between different forms of community membership are 'brokered' and reconciled to form one 'nexus' of identity, negotiability in shaping the meanings of the different communities of practice and negotiation of the relationship between membership of local communities of belonging and those at the macro level. Wenger (1998) argues that the community of practice model is useful for understanding aspects of identity such as gender, ethnicity and race. The work of Paechter (2003a, 2003b) has been particularly influential in examining how gender may be understood in this way. Ian's research examined the interplay and the tension which Wenger (1998) identifies as the children come to develop identities of participation or non-participation as members of the nursery and the local community and identities of full, partial or non-participation in the identities that are negotiated and renegotiated.

A number of studies point to the ways in which communities of practice need to be understood as emerging from the power dynamics of the tension between the micro and the macro. Holmes and Meyerhoff (1999) and Stapleton (2001, 2003) argue that the micro level community of practice can only be understood fully by reference to the macro, a view consistent with the stance in the present study. This is particularly evident in Ehrlich's (1999) study of a rape hearing and Ostermann's (2003) examination of the responses of female police officers to female victims where (male) political views and affiliations at the macro level come to affect the complexity of how identities are understood at the micro community of practice level and lead women to adopt the masculine discourses of the police and judiciary. In the nursery, despite the majority of the children and parents being of Pakistani heritage, those who hold power are of white indigenous heritage. It could be argued, as does Fleer (2003), that the emphasis on particular environments and provision and the significance of the dominant discourses of early childhood education form a particular community of practice, which emphasizes adult–child interaction and the importance of children's 'needs' (all of them constructed in a white, middle-class model) that 'are significant not only for what they explicitly produce, but also for what they silence and marginalize' (Ailwood 2003: 295). These were important matters to consider in a nursery where none of the children could readily be considered middle class and where very few of them were white.

Consistent with the above, Lineham and McCarthy (2000) argue that the dialogue between the individual and the community is not one of equals and that this has implications for the identities that are negotiated. A number of responses then become possible. Hodges (1998) illustrates how an individual may participate while experiencing 'dis-identification' because the individual's beliefs and world view do not sit easily with those who hold power and shape the dominant communities of practice. In contrast to the marginalization implicit in the above positions, Hodkinson and Hodkinson (2003) and Maynard (2001) argue that more account needs to be taken of how individual dispositions and responses affect and shape participation in communities of practice. Lineham and McCarthy (2000) and Renold (2004) draw usefully upon Davies and Harre's (1999) notion of 'positioning' to suggest that individuals have a far wider range of participation choices than suggested by Wenger (1998), with individuals being able 'to position themselves ... as well as ... being positioned by others through social interaction' (Renold 2004: 249). Thus, in Ian's research, interest began to focus, for example, on the way in which the dominant community of practice of the nursery school was acted out by a female staff that had white teachers in positions of power and staff of Pakistani heritage in the more junior positions. The dominant community of practice might be expected to seek to shape the identities that emerged and a key concern was to study the mechanisms by which this happened and the ways in which the children positioned themselves in relation to these expectations. National guidelines for early years education, for example, tend to mean that play and free choice for children are valued in some circumstances but children are also expected to respond to adult demands, often to ensure that they are learning how to 'behave appropriately' and making the expected progress in order to prepare them for what comes later, reflecting (male?) scientific notions of linear progress, development and conformity.

Ethnography and postmodernism

Bearing in mind the lack of existing literature regarding ethnic identity and young children, an ethnographic approach, underpinned by phenomenology, appeared the only tenable way in which to undertake the study. Such an approach finds support in the work of Corsaro and Molinari (2000: 180) who argue that 'ethnography is an ideal method ... particularly when it aims to both document children's evolving membership in their culture (Lave and Wenger 1991) and when focused on key transition points in children's lives'. It remains the case, however, as Gordon *et al.* (2001: 188) comment, that: 'ethnographic research with very young children has been sparse, and the lives of children have often been interpreted from adult perspectives'. In other words, there has been a tendency to privilege the views of adults and particularly male discourses of rationalism, against which children are seen as deficient and inadequate. Consequently, as James (1999: 248) also notes, much ethnographic research has focused on how adults teach children the lessons of culture, rather than 'how those lessons are learned by children'. The challenge was to attempt to engage with children's understandings and experiences as well as those of others in the communities of practice in which they participate.

Approaches to ethnography vary greatly but most have in common a concern to understand how people interpret the world and their experiences. They also tend to involve collecting very detailed descriptions of the field of study which are then used to generate theory. More recent approaches to ethnography (in contrast with earlier missionary and colonial versions) have also come to recognize the importance of an awareness of time, culture, society and politics in analysing the detailed descriptions. As Shaffir notes (1999), the generation of theory increasingly involves the researcher sharing his/her interpretation and theories with those studied and taking account of their views. As Rock comments (2001), much ethnographic work starts with an exploratory approach in which precise research questions and theories are not identified at the start but emerge from the detailed descriptions that have been gathered from work in the field. This point had particular resonance with Ian's attempts to explore the complexities of identity.

Ethnographic approaches have, in common with qualitative approaches more generally, been criticized on a number of grounds. The first is for a perceived lack of objectivity and rigour. It could be questioned, however, whether objectivity is actually ever possible. At the level of ontology, Ian's research started from the premise that social reality does not exist independently from those who create it, though, following Bhaskar (1998b) it has both a history and a future. At the level of epistemology, the stance is that the evidence which emerges from research can never consist of definite facts or knowledge. As Phillips (1993: 59) acknowledges, while criticizing qualitative approaches, 'nothing is known with such certainty that all possibility of future revision is removed. All knowledge is tentative.' In short, the study was located in a paradigm where what mattered was to strive for authenticity and where 'post-secular, post-critical, post-Enlightenment undecidability becomes not the last word, but the first in making room for something else to come about' (Lather 2001: 481).

As noted by Emerson *et al.* (2001), there is very little agreement among ethnographers regarding how to go about recording what happens in the field, yet this is important when considering the researcher's place within the research setting. While most ethnographers will agree that use is made of observation and field notes, there is little agreement about how these are undertaken. Some ethnographers make notes from the very beginning on the basis that by so doing they minimize the effect of note taking on those being observed. Emerson *et al.* (ibid: 357) assert, however, that 'Making open jottings ... reminds those studied that the fieldworker, despite constant proximity and frequent expressions of empathy, has radically different ... commitments and priorities ... '. While this may be the case the stance, in Ian's research, remained that any research is essentially a performance and a co-construction and a concern to seek to eliminate researcher effects by not taking notes seems to miss the point. It also seems an odd point for Emerson *et al.* (ibid: 353) to make, bearing in mind that they also comment that 'Field notes are a form of representation ... in

86

reducing the welter and confusion of the social world to written words, field notes (re)constitute that world in preserved forms'. As Van Maanen (1988: 8) makes clear, 'there is no direct correspondence between the world as experienced and the world as conveyed in a text'. While this may be the case, it is also important to recognize, as Hammersley and Atkinson (1995) note, that this does not mean that the relationship between the two is arbitrary but there is a sense, perhaps, in which the postmodern ethnography has 'a sort of stammering relation to its object' (Lather 2001: 487).

All of this pointed, for Ian, to the importance of a process of auto-ethnography as the means by which possible effects, meanings and understandings were explored. Once it is accepted that there can be no privileged place for the omniscient view of the researcher, what emerges is the writer's need to interrogate his/her own subjectivity (Goodley *et al.* 2004), the 'messy text' (Marcus 1994, cited in Plummer 2001) and 'an intense problematizing of the whole field' (Plummer 2001: 398). At the heart of this auto-ethnography was 'a strong reflexivity which recognizes that the ethnographer and his or her language are inevitably a part of the phenomenon that is being investigated' with 'a responsibility to recognize complexity and difference' (Spencer 2001: 450). However, as Coffey (1999: 18) notes, there is disagreement about the extent to which 'self-revelation and reflexivity' should appear in the analysis and a belief that 'the boundaries between self-indulgence and reflexivity are fragile and blurred' (ibid: 132) and often more personal insights appear only in the field notes and appendices. The auto-ethnography and the concern to engage with rather than create distance from the researched is consistent with the view of identities (those of children, staff and researcher) as social practice and as Maclure (2003: 156) notes 'the worlds of the ethnographer and subject start to seep into one another ... the assurance that comes from knowing one's Self in contrast to the Other begins to unravel'. Part of auto-ethnography, for Ian, was the need to engage with the unravelling in order to write the scripts of the researcher and the research. A significant part of the auto-ethnography was also a concern to interrogate the position of being a male researcher within the feminized world of early childhood education.

The incompetent (male) ethnographer

As discussed in the previous chapter, the home visits were intended to shed light on the environment of the home as the locus of practices and performances in relation to ethnic, gender and cultural identities. In visiting the homes, it was no easy matter to explain to the parents what the research was about. Many of the parents were not fluent in English, Ian does not speak Punjabi and a bilingual member of staff was not always available. In addition, there was the worry about how far the parents really felt they could refuse access and how this might relate to being visited by a white male, which was likely to be an unusual cultural occurrence. Even where parents were fluent in English, it was not always certain that they really understood what Ian was doing and in the early stages of the research the approach was exploratory and so Ian was not terribly clear either. As Murphy and Dingwall (2001: 342) argue: 'The ethical concerns raised by the opacity of sociological and anthropological interests to non-social scientists ... are further complicated by the emergent nature of research design and analysis in ethnography'.

Then there was the unease during the visits to the children's homes. These led Ian to question his ability to view the homes other than from a white, male, British, middle-class, educated perspective and made him conscious of the need to be aware of this lens. As Wenger comments (1998: 153):

> When we come in contact with new practices, we venture into unfamiliar territory. The boundaries of our communities manifest as a lack of competence ... we do not quite know how to engage with others. We do not understand the subtleties of the enterprise as the community has defined it.

Thus, as points of significance began to suggest themselves, Ian found that he was not comfortable in most of the homes, exploring social, cultural and religious worlds that he did not completely understand and it was not simply a case of being unfamiliar with the homes of people of Pakistani heritage. The world of religiosity (both Muslim and Christian) was as uncomfortable and unfamiliar as the degree of poverty experienced by some of the families. As Deegan (2001: 21) notes, this raises questions such as 'Can a stranger ever understand ... an "alien" culture? ... How important are differences between a sociologist and a subject if they vary by age, race, class, gender?'

The age of the children to be studied (3 years) posed particular issues in a number of respects. As Corsaro and Molinari (2000: 183) recognize, 'the ethnographer's acceptance into the world of children is particularly difficult because of obvious differences between adults and children in terms of cognitive and communicative maturity, power and physical size'. Until very recently, as Aubrey et al. note (1998), it has been considered by many researchers unnecessary to seek young children's consent, generally because of a belief that they are incapable of understanding and of offering a reasoned opinion. While more attention is now being given to issues of children's consent, genuinely informed consent is even more difficult than it is in the case of adults. In Ian's research, his approach was that, if studying individual children at close quarters, he sought their agreement and explained that he would be writing down what they were doing. This is not, however, to claim that there are any easy answers to questions of children's rights and consent. In the end, the main consideration had to be to satisfy himself that the children were not being exploited in the research.

This also involved, as James (1999) and Nilsen (2005) suggest that it should, seeking to use research methods which enabled the views of the children to be heard without intentionally or accidentally 'othering' them in the process. It required a complex model of what it means to listen to children's voices. The decision to study children's play, actions, paintings, drawings and choice of friends was a means of giving them a 'thickness of voice' that was made up of more than their words. This was considered particularly important in terms of addressing the language challenges posed by the age of the children and the status of many of them as speakers of English as an additional language.

A man in the nursery

On most occasions the children appeared to accept and understand Ian as another member of staff who was there to help them and talk to them. Thus he was called upon to help put on coats, deal with runny noses and was asked questions about where to find paper, aprons, scissors and so on. Often the children showed sophisticated under-standings about his needs and abilities. While observing a group of girls of Pakistani heritage playing with dolls and talking to each other in Punjabi, for example, the girls became aware of Ian's presence and started to speak English instead, realizing that he would not be able to understand what they were saying. While observing children at the sand tray, the conversation was often in Punjabi but would very rapidly switch to English when there were disagreements over equipment that the children wanted Ian to resolve. However, as Measor and Woods (1991: 67) noted, 'children are capable of ... constructing a world in which the distinction between what grown ups can and cannot hear is important' and, on a small number of occasions, Punjabi appeared to be used as a means of keeping Ian (and members of the nursery staff) outside the children's community of practice.

At the beginning of Ian's time in the nursery school, it was particularly the white boys who sought his attention. Often they followed him around and sometimes would simply stand by his side and gaze at him. Questions were raised about how far gender identification was significant in these behaviours in the way that Freud (1991) or Lacan (1989) might suggest. Did Ian simply pay more attention to the boys than to the girls? Did the boys find themselves in a feminized environment that they did not quite understand and so looked to Ian to help them make sense of the environment? As time went by these boys were less interested in Ian's presence but were replaced by boys of Pakistani heritage. Did Ian's white skin colour mean that the boys of Pakistani heritage did not initially identify with him but that gender identification became a factor for them as the weeks progressed? Did Ian unwittingly pay more attention to the boys of white indigenous heritage who then responded accordingly, leaving the boys of Pakistani heritage feeling excluded initially? Did they lack experience of playing alongside white children and not feel able to approach Ian until the boys of white indigenous heritage had withdrawn?

Very rarely did the children show any concern about Ian's presence in the nursery but there were a very small number of instances where this was the case. It could be suggested that some of this anxiety was caused by Ian's presence as a male adult alongside an all-female staff in the nursery but it was never clear that this was the reason. In the first year of data collection a girl of white indigenous heritage was very anxious whenever Ian was in her vicinity and cast sideways glances and often ran off to other activities. Ian spoke to her mother about this and she confirmed that her daughter did tend to be nervous in the presence of men and always hid when her uncle visited her home. Ian tried to maintain what he thought the girl considered a safe distance and, with time and familiarity, she did seem to become more accepting of his presence but there was still a feeling that there was an abuse of power involved, however unintentional. In the second year of data collection a girl of Pakistani heritage, Sadaf, became very agitated whenever she was aware that Ian was in the nursery. Initially, she had seemed to enjoy his presence in story times, smiling at him at regular intervals. With hindsight, perhaps this was actually indicative of anxiety and her smiles very quickly changed to tears. Normally a happy and confident child, according to the nursery staff, she immediately became tearful as soon as she realized that he was in the building. At Christmas, she was Mary in the school's nativity and Ian spent much of the time hiding from her but she spotted him towards the end of the performance and once again became very upset. The bilingual staff tried to find out why she was upset by Ian's presence, but she was unable to explain. Her main concern was just that Ian should not go to her story time. There was disagreement among the staff about whether Ian should respect these concerns or whether she needed 'to get used to men for later on at school'.

Sadaf's reaction was unsettling for Ian because he had

always found that young children responded well to him and he found himself saying so to members of staff, in an attempt to justify and feel better about the situation. It also raised new questions about how identities might be understood. As someone who had studied and worked for many years in environments that were always almost entirely populated by women, Ian saw himself primarily as someone who works with young children, rather than as a man in an otherwise all-female environment who works with young children. In other words, for Ian, conventional notions of gender and sexual identity were not significant aspects of how he saw himself in the workplace. If gender really was a factor here, this led to important considerations for Ian. It would raise questions about his whole sense of identity as an early childhood practitioner and researcher if gender identity was significant and Ian was not aware of it. If, however, Ian's identity is not primarily dictated by gender, then this leads to further considerations. The first is whether there were other aspects of Ian's identity and persona that were significant and what these might be. The second is that if Sadaf's experiences of fixing in relation to gender were such that she was able to view Ian only in that way, then there are clear implications for the sort of work that might be necessary with Sadaf to enable her to move beyond the fixings.

Throughout the two years that Ian spent observing in the nursery, there were a small number of boys of white indigenous heritage who sought Ian's attention on a regular basis and also made it difficult to observe the other children. These were often boys who were considered by staff to present challenging behaviour. This raised questions about how such boys became seen as badly behaved and about why they turned to Ian. Did the all female staff have expectations that were particularly difficult for some boys? Certainly nurseries, and schools more generally, tend to see well-adjusted children as those who sit, work and play quietly and comply with adult requests and these boys did not approach their time in nursery in this way. Was the interest in Ian based on gender identification and, if so, what were the origins of feeling that someone of the same sex would be more sympathetic? Certainly, as a male who was always well-behaved and studious, Ian was intrigued and slightly disconcerted by this attention. Was it because, as a visitor, Ian was seen as less aware of past issues and more likely to respond in a positive manner? As the children entered the nursery, Ian would seek to make notes about what they did on arrival but one boy, Brian, would come straight up and attempt to take the note pad and pen and say, 'Put it there', wanting Ian to slap hands with him. Knowing that the staff would not encourage this, and not being the type of greeting with which Ian was comfortable anyway, he did not feel that this was something that could be encouraged. On other occasions, as Ian sat in the construction area with his note pad next to him, Brian would pick it up and say that he was going to do some writing. On the one hand, Ian felt he should be able to do this but, on the other hand, knew that the staff would see it as part of his challenging behaviour which should not be encouraged. There was also the nagging suspicion that they were making judgements about how the behaviour was handled. Ian felt that this was a recurring theme going back to his time as head teacher. At that time, it was based on some differences of opinion about how children should be treated and on the unusual situation of having a male head teacher in a nursery school. During the research, newer members of staff appeared interested in how a man was dealing with the children's behaviour while staff who Ian had previously worked with were more interested in what appeared to be seen as the expert opinion from a university academic, though perhaps

shaded with questions about the practical skills of someone who no longer worked directly with children.

Ian's insider/outsider role was, in fact, a key part of the
research experience. A degree of 'outsiderness' was useful in seeing afresh how identities were enacted but there
was also the 'insiderness' of old professional and personal
identities and relationships being re-enacted, though, of
course, not quite as they were with a time lapse of ten
years. While there was a concern to try to reserve judgement in the research, this proved difficult. The staff cast
Ian in the role of expert and sought his views and opinions at every turn, in the manner noted by Hammersley
and Atkinson (1995). Leaving houses, 'verdicts' were
sought and Ian attempted to deflect the questions back to
the members of staff and to cast them as expert in their
own community but this tended to lead to a feeling that
they had been let down in some way. Ian would sit quietly
in the staff meeting and suddenly be asked to talk about
what he had observed and whether they were 'doing
anything wrong'. It points to questions about who is
'expert' in any community and why. Did the status stem
from being an academic, from being the ex-head teacher
(but then the present head teacher sought similar verdicts), or simply from being male in the feminized world
of the nursery school? All these are important considerations because, as Ball (1993: 36) identifies:

> The nature, limitations, and possibilities of data can be fully
> appreciated only when we ... know how the actors' percep-
> tions of the researcher have influenced what they have and
> have not said and done. Naïve claims about blending into
> the scene are not enough to convince an informed reader
> that the problem of the research role has been solved.

All this led to a feeling that Ian was not quite sure what he
was doing or what his role was or should be. He often felt

quite incapable of talking to the staff in any meaningful way about what he was finding. There was a certain unease in trying to negotiate a relationship with the staff in which Ian somehow felt the need to try to make sure they still recognized that he was the person who had been the head teacher (perhaps because of a perception that some of them were sceptical about the value of research and of academia) but at the same time being aware that he had become someone else. As well as what they did not know about him in terms of his new life as an academic, there was also what they did know. They knew that he had recently moved from the area and had never liked living there. What did that mean in terms of the experiences and context that was now being researched? Did they think the concern was to criticize and make fun?

In order to help deal with these matters, as well as to try to take account of as many points of view as possible, Ian routinely shared what seemed significant aspects of the fieldwork with the staff in the nursery school and sought their interpretation and shared his own. Thus the auto-ethnography that emerged sought to represent different points of view and multiple tellings. However, that multiple tellings are opened up does not remove the issue, as Murphy and Dingwall (2001) note, that the multiple tellings are those of the ethnographer. It remains true that the auto-ethnography remains Ian's understanding of what they said and his selective representation of it. By using auto-ethnography, he sought at least to make explicit that it was his interpretation and did not seek to establish an invisible authority for the interpretations. As Spencer advocates (2001: 450), Ian sought to 'recognize complexity and difference, rather than hide them beneath a veil of homogeneity and generalization' and attempted to represent these differing viewpoints in the written account, but this is not the same as saying that he necessarily accepted their viewpoints and portrayed matters wholly as they saw them. As Murphy and Dingwall (2001: 342) recognize, this 'stance may be experienced as betrayal or rejection by participants who expect researchers to affirm or endorse their version'. This was a particular issue given that Ian knew the staff so well and the best he could hope to do was to ensure that they understood that he would necessarily 'reframe their versions' (ibid: 346).

Grappling with research

All this points to the complexities of carrying out research. Questions are raised about whether Ian could ever hope to understand the identities that were enacted in the nursery because of the difficulties of becoming a part of the communities of practice of the children (and that was impossible because of differences relating to matters such as power, age, class, race and religion) and of the adults and children (and that was impossible as an semi-insider/outsider who only became a part of that community at particular times). There was also the danger that in becoming even a partial insider as part of those communities of practice, Ian would find himself 'going native' and run the risk of seeing things only from the same perspective as the staff. Part of Ian's response was to use auto-ethnography as a means of thinking his way into the actions, thoughts and beliefs of communities that he could not always experience at first hand and where there appeared to be multiple factors at work in any situation. While he could not know that he had understood enactment of identities in the ways in which the participants had, and could not be sure of what his part had been in the enactment of those identities, he could at least seek to engage in numerous and contrasting analyses while recognizing that what was recorded and analysed could only ever be personal, selective and partial. In so doing, Ian's research 'generates blind spots and defers consensus' (Lyotard 1984: 61) but, in so doing, as Clarke (2005) proposes, there is a commitment to multiple readings of seemingly established concepts and situations to open up other possibilities of understanding the complexity of the ways in which children's identities are lived and performed.

6

Research as Performance and Practice

Introduction

The last chapter began to point to the complexities of researcher identities in the field. This chapter seeks to explore how the context in which any piece of research is carried out may be viewed as one where performances are enacted. The performative aspect of research is seen as involving shifting and dynamic stagings in relation to multiple boundaries of context, power relations, point in history, time of year, day of the week, ability, gender, race, culture, class and religion. In Ian's research about identity in a particular nursery school, the performative nature of research and identity was particularly apparent at plastic and permeable boundary moments related to special occasions, such as visiting children at home, staff–parent conferences, school trips and celebrations such as Eid and Christmas where the masks of children, staff and Ian as the researcher often appeared ill-fitting and shifting and slipped to give a glimpse of identities behind, between and beyond. This notion of fluid but dyspraxic performance may be seen to take us to the very limits of the comfortable and raises questions about what we can possibly hope to find out in a world of multiple realities. It raises questions about

> the boundaries that research conjures, and maintains, in order to produce truth, certainty and authenticity –

boundaries between representation and reality, sincerity and pretence, rational and irrational ... self and other ... The possibility of any breach in those boundaries is ... generally treated as a threat to be contained, lest mischief and paradox should be unleashed upon an orderly world (Maclure 2003: 149).

The focus of this chapter will be to provide an exploration of ways to treat 'mischief and paradox' as phenomena 'to be engaged rather than evaded'.

Research, truth, fiction and performance

Viewing the research process as performative could suggest that it is being claimed that all research involves a fiction in which there is only one story to be told. Traditional approaches to research have certainly tried to claim that there is only one 'story' but the concern has been to avoid any 'contamination' by fiction, espousing scientific claims to objectivity, truth and fact. More recent approaches, as we have seen in earlier chapters, have disputed that there are absolute facts and truths to be discovered through research and have begun to challenge the usefulness of the truth/fiction binary and to argue for the importance of recognizing the performative aspects of identities, social reality and research (see e.g., Denzin and Lincoln 1995; Lather 2001 and Maclure 2003). In the theatre, fiction is readily accepted and we are invited to see and experience it as truth in order to understand more about ourselves and the nature of our lives. It is also true, perhaps, that the staging of plays has often tended to curtail and contain any notion of multiple tellings and variations and has attempted to construct a single, supposedly logical and coherent account in the interests of control, causality and some notion of singular ways of understanding. In relation to common approaches to ethnography (the underpinning methodology in Ian's research), Maclure (2003) argues that the approach has often been suggestive of non- fiction travel writing and has been cinematic. She goes on to note (ibid: 91) that 'the guidebook format, the panoramic perspective and the fixed vantage point' are concerned with boundary maintenance in a filmic portrayal of the world that privileges the director/researcher over the actors and audience/those being researched. Even where attempts are made to 'get inside' and to use the voices of the researched, there is usually still a concern with boundary between self and other, between real and unreal, between the natural and the made up. There is often a conviction that actors and those whose lives we touch upon in order to carry out research are 'making it up', 'not being themselves', but this assumes that there is only one self to be while the self that appears in the performances (whether at the theatre or in the research context) is one of many selves, the self or selves which appear in that particular context under those conditions. Other selves appear under other conditions but those other selves are also performances and are not necessarily any more 'real'.

If one accepts the performative, illusory nature of reality and of research, then one needs to go much further than has been common in reducing the distance between director, actors and audience/researcher and researched. Trying to get inside actors' heads, removing the proscenium arch and performing in the round with less distance between the director, actors and audience may enable more perspectives and greater closeness, but all too often it is taken for granted as meaning that there is more likelihood of the play being understood in the same way, when there is no reason to believe that this is so. In a similar fashion, greater closeness between researcher and researched may ensure that multiple interpretations are accounted for but it does not mean there is one way of understanding the performance or that one can be found. Research performances need to be reconceptualized as involving casting and recasting as roles are negotiated, assigned, contested and renegotiated. The possibility of multiple tellings and shifting performances needs to be recognized as the stagings reflect the different interpretations of the different people involved from different perspectives. These multiple tellings reflect a belief that this is the nature of how the world is and the contention, therefore, is that research can no longer satisfy itself with a single unproblematic narrative. We all act out different beings in different situations with different others and to seek to eliminate these 'performances' is to eliminate what there is to be known, to reduce the multiple to a false and restricting unity that leaves no place for the spaces in between that give us some sense of glimpsing the nodal points between apparently discontinuous performances. The context in which any piece of research is carried out can indeed be viewed as one or more performances but these need to be understood as faltering and ungainly co-productions that involve improvisation in response to new situations as well as carefully framed scripting and direction that bear witness to the reproductive nature of the *habitus*. The art of the director/researcher in this context is to conjure scripts and analyses of the performances that are as authentic from as many perspectives as possible, not in order to seek one truth but to recognize that there are many. Auto-ethnography (see Chapter 5) was used in Ian's research as a means of troubling and problematizing certainties and of opening up multiple readings and interpretations of surface performances and actions in order to better understand what might be significant and what might be beneath.

Exploring performances and meanings through auto-ethnography

Auto-ethnography is an unsettling business and one that involves the researcher in a stream of multiple tellings that can be uncomfortable and personally troubling. Despite an awareness that reality, whatever it might mean, is multi-layered, in Ian's research about ethnic, gender and class identities he often found himself struggling to remain open to the different possibilities that might be at play because of a nagging commitment to some form of 'greater good' or feeling that some decisions are more defendable than others. During Ian's time as head teacher of the nursery, when 50 per cent of the nursery was of Pakistani heritage, there had been heated debates over the tradition of staging the nativity as part of the Christmas concert and an uneasy suspension had been agreed upon. Returning as a researcher ten years later, this was still a disputed matter. The nativity performance had been reinstated even though 80 per cent of the children were now of Pakistani heritage. In seeking to understand the views of staff, rather than impose a directorial interpretation that would suggest thoughtlessness or worse on the part of the staff, Ian spoke first to the head teacher. She explained that the staff had been discussing the meaning of Christmas in a nursery attended by a majority of Muslim children but said that the dilemma was really that most of the staff were practising Christians who attended church regularly and felt that their beliefs were compromised if they did not give the children opportunities to understand and celebrate the meaning of Christmas. In discussion with the rest of the staff, however, a number of them said they were concerned (despite their faith) that, by reading stories about Christmas presents, many of the children might be disappointed if they did not receive them. Questions are raised perhaps about the extent to which attention to the needs and vulnerabilities of the children might be used by staff as justification for compromising their beliefs. Two of the three teachers questioned the time devoted to Christmas while the nursery nurses felt that the time and celebrations were appropriate. Ian had expected the bilingual assistants to see the festivities as inappropriate but they did not. Perhaps the concerns of the teachers but not of the bilingual assistants point to the ways in which suggesting resistance is easier for those with more power, while those with less power learn to perform what they perceive the dominant culture expects and come to perceive this as part of who they are.

The inadequacy of seeking a single reading or interpretation was highlighted further, in Ian's research, by the views of the bilingual assistants. One of them felt that the parents do not mind Christmas activities at nursery and expect there to be celebrations even though they do not share the beliefs, because they have come to understand the significance that Christmas has in schools. Another bilingual nursery nurse said, in relation to the performance of the nativity, that she did not think it was problematic for the children or their families because Jesus is recognized as a prophet in Islam and so the story is relevant for them and does not run counter to their beliefs, provided that Jesus is not referred to as the son of God. She said that Christmas was celebrated in an increasing number of Muslim homes because of the influence of television, the shops and what the children experience in school. She also said that even though her family take their Muslim faith very seriously, her niece and nephew had a Christmas tree and received Christmas presents each year. In this sense, Christmas was 'performed' in growing numbers of Muslim homes as a cultural but non-religious festival. It is useful to bear in mind Butler's (1999) contention here that the illusion of fixed and essential internalized identities is created through culturally and politically regulated, repeated and stylized performances that are 'instituted through acts which are internally discontinuous ... the *appearance of substance* is precisely that ... a performative accomplishment which the social audience, including the actors themselves, come to believe and to perform in the mode of belief' (1999: 179, author's emphasis). The presence of multiple tellings here, which appear at times contradictory, points to the way in which she also argues that occasional failures of repetition and stylization reveal the ways in which identities are illusory.

There were other occasions in Ian's research when negotiation of the meaning of performances was contested. There were times when, despite his concern to avoid the 'panoramic perspective and the fixed vantage point' (Maclure 2003: 91), he fell into precisely these traps. Each visit to the nursery began with a description of the nursery environment and this extract from the ethnography points to the dangers:

> *Almost all of the display boards are covered with Christmas cards that the children have made. These consisted of: red cards with white snowmen on; blue cards with silver mesh stars and purple dots; red, blue and yellow cards with glitter stars; triangles in many different colours with circles and glitter on; blue and black cards with two circles, sand, glitter, red feathers and red sticks to make robins and blue cards with pink skin-coloured hand prints with faces on to make reindeer but the majority of the children do not have pink skin!!*

Discussing the reindeer with the staff, they told Ian that the faces were the children's self-portraits. Ian's immediate interpretation of the pink-faced reindeer was that the staff had been thoughtless in not taking account of the brown skin colour of the majority of the children when providing the children with the paint. Truth, reality, fiction and justification are all highly debatable, however, and the concern to construct a shared understanding of the meanings of the performances in the nursery appeared to lead to layer upon layer of further possibilities and a contested and uneasy struggle to establish meanings. The staff suggested that the faces were not intended to be pink and simply reflected what had happened when the brown for the reindeers' faces had been placed on to blue card. Questions are opened up about how the staff viewed Ian in this situation and there was certainly an apparent concern to challenge any directorial control that Ian might have in this situation, partly, perhaps, on the basis of challenging an academic reading with a practical one, an outsider view with an insider one. In not taking account of the practical aspect of paint mixing, it could be argued that the staff sought to wrestle for control of the performance. In not entering sufficiently into the community of nursery practice, Ian found himself marginalized from it and his views not considered legitimate.

The contested diasporic spaces of research

Research relationships are, therefore, conceived of as performances that are enacted in the diaspora spaces (Brah 1996) of ever-shifting patterns of behaviour and meaning-making in relation to the performers, the context, discourses of power and the occasion of the boundary. Research has many of the same qualities drawn attention to by Cavarero (2000) when she argues that identity is contextual, unstable, sporadic, incomplete, transitory and often apparently the result of chance 'because the weaving-work of memory' (p. 35) has the same qualities. She goes on to argue that identity is relational and is constructed through one's actions and through the (desired) narrating of one's actions under the necessary gaze of others. Research activities and meanings are thus conceived of as being performed in these diaspora spaces 'where belonging and otherness is appropriated and contested ... individuals and collectivities are simultaneously positioned in social relations constituted and performed across multiple dimensions of differentiation' (Brah 1996: 242–3). Research relationships are viewed as 'complex mixtures of power and dependence ... expertise and helplessness ... authority and collegiality ... resistance and compliance ... trust and suspicion, friendship and hatred' (Wenger 1998: 77). The sense that can be made in any research situation is viewed as a performance, a representation of certain elements of that research context, depending on the continuities, discontinuities, common ground and boundaries between the researcher and those in the research situation. Research, therefore, is negotiated and performed in particular communities amidst discourses of power, heritage, present circumstances and through the things that we see and do not see, through the things that are said and not said by ourselves and others, through the things that happen or do not happen, through the things that we do or do not do, through the things to which we pay attention and through the things to which we do not. Research activities are therefore not single performances, a unity, but many and disparate, contested and uncontested, relational and interactive, unrelated and fractured. Following Foucault (2002) power operates within research communities to suggest the value of particular research performances in which meanings are tenuously stitched together in time from the splintering, the ambiguities, the places between, the excluded and the overlaps of the difference and deferral implied in the hybridity of the borderline. The allocation of meanings in research is understood as circumstantial, negotiated and renegotiated, concerned with 'absent presence' (Nayak 2006: 415) and *différance* in Derrida's sense (2002) of both difference and deferral and as involving 'the intricacies, paradoxes, dilemmas, contradictions, imperatives, superficialities, and profundities of the way individuals relate to and are related to the world in which they live' (Verkuyten 2005: 42).

Research and communities of practice

Viewing research as involving performances in the field in this way highlights the ways in which the practices and outcomes of research are not in any way straight forward. We have already seen that performances are complex and multiple. If Ian had entered further into the community of nursery practice, questions could be raised about a particularly significant performance in which Ian was engaged: that of researcher. What is being suggested is that there may be a tension between researcher identity as part of the academy and researcher identity as part of the field of action. As noted earlier, a key challenge of qualitative research is often considered to be to avoid 'going native' and being unable to see what is important in a research situation. This, however, supposes that subjectivity is avoidable and undesirable and a place of privilege in relation to some supposedly objective form of observation and interpretation that does not sit easily with the stance being developed here.

It could be further argued that, as well as the performance that is enacted in the field between researcher and those involved in research, there are other parallel performances. There are, for example, other performances in relation to nursery education in places near and far that could be seen to form a community of practice concerning the principles and practices of early child-hood education. Hodkinson (2004) also argues that research activities and researchers themselves can be seen as making up a community of practice in terms of the characteristics identified by Wenger (1998): mutual engagement (in handling diversity and difference in order to create a shared way of doing things); joint enterprise (involving negotiation, co-ordination, mutual accountability); and a shared repertoire (of experiences, discourses, stories, history, styles). Research activities and meanings are seen as being experienced and performed through involvement in communities of research practice that include identification, negotiatibility and reification of researcher identities as practice trajectories that link with other researchers in other locations through engagement, imagination and alignment and the possi-bilities of participation and non-participation.

This brings us to the need to consider the ways in which meanings are established through the research process. Hammersley (2005) argues that conceptualizing research as a community of practice is not adequate in that the notion of situated learning pays insufficient attention to the significance of 'systematic reflection, of the kind associated with science' (p. 17) but he refers to the earlier work by Lave and Wenger (1991) and Lave (1996) rather than to Wenger (1998), who discusses learning and understanding as emanating from 'economies of mean-ing'. Hammersley's stance (2005) tends to privilege cer-tain ways of knowing and does not appear to recognize that systematic reflection is a construct, one that has emerged from the Enlightenment and views the logical and scientific as the only way of understanding the world. Wenger (1998) helps us to understand that such con-ceptions are constructs which emerge from economies of meaning that are made up of: a social system of relative values, which lead to meanings having different degrees of currency; the negotiated character of these relative values, with participants having differential degrees of control over meanings that are produced; the possibility of accumulating ownership of meaning, with the constant possibility of such positions being contested; and systems of legitimation in relation to the processes of negotiation. In short, the significance of logical and scientific thought is only that it has developed a privileged place in ways of understanding the world. This does not mean that it is the only way.

In this sense, certain ways of thinking and understanding are more likely to emerge than others, not necessarily because they are 'true' but because they carry the imprint of the operation of power in determining what is important and how it is to be understood. The tension remains here in relation to researcher identity in the academy and researcher identity and meaning relationships in the field. The negotiation of economies of meaning in the field may be at odds with the orthodoxy of the academy, creating a crisis of legitimacy. However much a researcher may feel that economies of meaning negotiated in the field are significant to understanding that situation, researchers also face the necessity of needing to square these with a need to achieve legitimacy in the academy for academic, professional and financial reasons. Writing about ethnography, Van Maanen (1988: 25) draws attention to the ways in which research is always written 'with particular audiences in mind and reflect(s) the presumptions carried by authors regarding the attitudes, expectations, and backgrounds of their intended readers'. Research contracts, funding bodies, responding to significant research traditions, strategic university priorities, government requirements, the predilections of particular journals and of examiners all shape the ways in which researcher identities are shaped, maintained and renegotiated. Thus researchers may find themselves performing research identities as though appearing to believe in them while actually feeling compromised by the performances that are required of them. Hodkinson (2004) suggests that Wenger (1998) does not pay sufficient attention to situations such as these where individuals engage legitimately in practice but do not actually identify with the values and beliefs of the community of practice. Hodges' (1998) notion of 'dis-identification', which she identifies among beginning teachers in relation to professional and regulatory requirements while appearing to take part in the practices of the teaching community, is helpful in understanding the ways in which researcher identities may be experienced. It is also helpful in understanding how identities may be experienced among those with whom research is being carried out. In Ian's research, there were certainly moments where the children gained status as legitimate participants in the nursery community of practice but appeared not to identify with it. Mitchell, for example, was a legitimate participant in celebrating Eid in the nursery, but said that he would not be doing so at home 'because we're not dark, are we?' Zil-Huma took a significant part in the nativity performance while also telling a white nursery nurse that she must not wear mendhi because 'you're a white woman'. Some of the staff of white indigenous origin also celebrated Christmas with the children while not believing it was the right thing to do.

The futility of research?

If all performances, whether those involved in carrying out research or those that enact life more generally, are illusory, but carried out in the manner of belief, then there is a danger, in the argument so far developed, that there appears to be no point in carrying out research. As Sayer (1998) argues, however, this is not to claim that any performance and any explanation will do as well as any other and it is argued that critical realist perspectives are seen as enabling us to treat 'mischief and paradox' as phenomena 'to be engaged rather than evaded' (Maclure 2003: 149). Bhaskar (1998b) claims that the social world pre-exists people and cannot be reduced simply to human agents and actions but is not independent of them. At the same time, the maintenance and transformation of the materials, relations, values and beliefs of society depend on human agency and activity and, therefore, are situational and temporal. The form that this agency can take in reproducing, understanding and transforming is itself constrained by social structures but these social structures are in turn to be understood as social products which are subject to change and 'so may be only relatively enduring' (Bhaskar 1998a: 218). The effects of these structures can be seen in everyday life but there is no one-to-one relationship between effects, causes and structures and there may be numerous effects with numerous causes. The notion that there are effects that can be seen, however, leads Bhaskar (1998c) to argue that there must be pre-existing causal structures. Causes are viewed by Bhaskar (1998a) as tendencies rather than as certainties and their effects may not be seen or even actually occur. In other words, as Outhwaite notes (1998: 291) 'we can ask ... what a given society must be like in order for people to behave within it, and to conceive it, in the ways they do'.

Critical realist perspectives maintain that a key concern is to provide an adequate account of observable effects because an inadequate conceptualization of effects will lead to difficulties in seeking to understand the causal tendencies that underpin them. This, however, has to be achieved in a world where the researcher encounters heterogeneous discourses ... entering into conversations, noticing sites and images along the way, gathering stories and available 'collectibles' ... The researcher wanders about asking questions and reconstructs the answers as new stories to be told of his or her adventures. Post-modern knowledge is validated through practice(s). The post-modern is complicated, impure, messy, full of different kinds of 'stuff' that the researcher collected and now must somehow handle – rather like life itself (Clarke 2005: 166).

In order to seek to examine these performances in ways that allow for exploration of 'causal tendencies', Clarke (ibid) proposes a model of analysis based on the use of situational maps. These are intended to identify all the elements in the situation and examine the relationships between them, first in messy and then in ordered and relational forms. In parallel, she promotes the use of social worlds/arenas maps (which identify all the meso and macro level influences and their discourses in the social worlds and arenas and the boundary markers between them), and positional maps (which chart the different positions taken and the spaces and silences between them without reference to the identification of individual or collective voices). There are dangers, however, that mapping may lead to formulaic analysis and to fixed positions being marked out. Clarke maintains that these are tendencies to be avoided and that the concern is not with singular readings or with purity but with representing the field of possibilities. In this regard, the model is considered useful to establishing the multiple and messy analyses but the mapping elements do carry these dangers, particularly in the case of positional maps, where Clarke conceives of positions as being mapped along axes. While the axes are intended to help conceive of a continuum, the positions reflect polar opposites in ways that return to defining a binary, which Clarke has argued against.

As within critical realism, Clarke argues that situations are 'rooted' in notions of the underlying world. While Clarke uses the root metaphor, she actually draws attention, in the same way that Bhaskar and Lawson (1998) do, to how what is needed is an analysis of the ways in which there may be multiple causes and effects that cannot be linked together in any singular manner: 'There are no one-way arrows, but instead attempts to delineate processes of co-constitution through specifying conditions and relationalities' (Clarke 2005: 298). In this sense, it may be more helpful to think once again not in terms of links back to roots but rather in terms of rhizomatic relationships (Deleuze and Guattari 2004) that can be broken at any point but that 'will start up again on one of its old lines, or on new lines' (ibid: 10), which will still be 'part of the rhizome' and 'tie back to one another' (ibid).

Peering between the gaps

The sense that can be made in any research situation is, therefore, viewed as emerging from shifting performances which provide glimpses of something beneath and between them and evidence of underlying tendencies, representations of certain but not necessarily all elements of that research context. While we can seek to research carefully, there is no claim that the same findings will emerge if someone else carries out the research or even if the same researcher carries it out again, because the surface features of any act of production are likely to represent some elements but not others in relation to what lies behind them and there may be other performances that are missing or do not occur during any piece of research. Different directors, actors and audiences will emphasize and recognize different features as being significant and different stage sets will cast different light and shadow on the appearance of substance. The research process is, therefore, to be understood as the endless search to capture what is present, what is absent and what is only glimpsed in the performance and to trace the splintering shoots of the rhizomatic meanings and explanations on the surface, beneath, above, behind and between.

References

Aboud, F. (1988) *Children and Prejudice*, Oxford: Blackwell.

Adler, S. M. (2001) 'Racial and ethnic identity formation of midwestern Asian-American children', *Contemporary Issues in Early Childhood*, 2, (3), 265–94.

Ailwood, J. (2003) 'Governing early childhood through play', *Contemporary Issues in Early Childhood*, 4, (3), 286–99.

Alcoff, L. (1988) 'Cultural feminism versus post-structuralism: the identity crisis in feminist theory', *Signs: Journal of Women in Culture and Society*, 13, (31), 405–37.

Apple, M. (2001) *Educating the 'Right' Way: Markets, Standards, God and Inequality*, New York: RoutledgeFalmer.

Archer, J. and Lloyd, B. (2002) *Sex and Gender*, Cambridge: Cambridge University Press.

Archer, L. and Yamashita, H. (2003) 'Theorising inner-city masculinities: "race", class, gender and education', *Gender and Education*, 15, (2) 115–32.

Askew, S. and Ross, C. (1988) *Boys Don't Cry: Boys and Sexism in Education*, Milton Keynes: Open University Press.

Aubrey, C., David, T., Godfrey, R. and Thompson, L. (2000) *Early Childhood Educational Research: Issues in Methodology and Ethics*, London: RoutledgeFalmer.

Ball, S. J. (1993) 'Self-doubt and soft data: social and technical trajectories in ethnographic fieldwork' in M. Hammersley (ed.), *Educational Research: Current Issues*, London: Paul Chapman.

Baron-Cohen, S. (2003) *Men, Women and the Extreme Male Brain*, London: Penguin.

Barry, P. (1995) *Beginning Theory: An Introduction to Literary and Cultural Theory*, Manchester: Manchester University Press.

Barth, F. (1966) *Models of Social Organisation*, Occasional Paper no. 23, London: Royal Anthropological Institute.

Barth, F. (ed.) (1969) *Ethnic Groups and Boundaries: The Social Organisation of Culture Difference*, Oslo: Universitetsforlaget.

Bhaskar, R. (1998a) 'Philosophy and scientific realism' in M. Archer, R. Bhaskar, A. Collier, T. Lawson and A. Norrie (eds), *Critical Realism: Essential Readings*, London: Routledge.

Bhaskar, R. (1998b) 'Societies' in M. Archer, R. Bhaskar, A. Collier, T. Lawson and A. Norrie (eds), *Critical Realism: Essential Readings*, London: Routledge.

Bhaskar, R. (1998c) 'The logic of scientific discovery' in M. Archer, R. Bhaskar, A. Collier, T. Lawson and A. Norrie (eds), *Critical Realism: Essential Readings*, London: Routledge.

Bhaskar, R. and Lawson, T. (1998) 'Introduction: basic texts and developments' in M. Archer, R. Bhaskar, A. Collier, T. Lawson and A. Norrie (eds), *Critical Realism: Essential Readings*, London: Routledge.

Bhatti, G. (1999) *Asian Children at Home and at School*, London: Routledge.

Biddulph, S. (1998) *Raising Boys: Why Boys are Different – and How to Help Them Become Happy and Well-balanced Men*, Sydney: Finch.

Boldt, G. (2002) 'Oedipal and other conflicts', *Contemporary Issues in Early Childhood*, 3, (3), 365–82.

Boler, M. (1999) *Feeling Power: Emotions and Education*, London: Routledge.

Brah, A. (1996) *Cartographies of Diaspora: Contesting Identities*, London: Routledge.

Bronfenbrenner, U. (1979) *The Ecology of Human Development: Experiments by Nature and Design*, Cambridge, MA: Harvard University Press.

Brooker, L. (2002) *Starting School: Young Children Learning Cultures*, Buckingham: Open University Press.

Brown, T. and Jones, L. (2001) *Action Research and Postmodernism: Congruence and Critique*, Buckingham: Open University Press.

Burman, E. (1994) *Deconstructing Developmental Psychology*, London: Routledge.

Burman, E. (1999) 'Morality and the goals of development' in M. Woodhead, M. D. Faulkner and K. Littleton (eds), *Making Sense of Social Development*, London: Routledge.

Butler, J. (1990) 'Gender trouble, feminist theory and psychoanalytic discourse' in L. Nicholson (ed.), *Feminism/Postmodernism*, London: Routledge.

Butler, J. (1993) *Bodies that Matter: On the Discursive Limits of 'Sex'*, London: Routledge.

Butler, J. (1999) *Gender Trouble: Feminism and the Subversion of Identity*, (2nd edn), London: Routledge.

Butler, J. (2004) 'Bodily inscriptions, performative subversions' in S. Salih with J. Butler (eds), *The Judith Butler Reader*, Oxford: Blackwell.

Cannella, G. S. and Viruru, R. (2004) *Childhood and Postcolonization: Power, Education and Contemporary Practice*, New York: RoutledgeFalmer.

Cavarero, A. (2000) *Relating Narratives: Storytelling and Selfhood*, London: Routledge.

Cixous, H. (1987) 'Sorties' in H. Cixous and C. Clément (eds), *The Newly Born Woman*, Manchester: Manchester University Press.

Clarke, A. (2005) *Situational Analysis: Grounded Theory After the Postmodern Turn*, London: Sage.

Clarricoates, K. (1978) 'Dinosaurs in the classroom: a re-examination of some aspects of the hidden curriculum in primary schools', *Women's Studies International Quarterly*, 1, (4), 353–64.

Coffey, A. (1999) *The Ethnographic Self: Fieldwork and the Representation of Identity*, London: Sage.

Connell, R. (1989) 'Cool guys, swots and wimps: the interplay of masculinity and education', *Oxford Review of Education*, 15, (3), 291–303.

Connolly, P. (1995) 'Racism, masculine peer-group relations and the schooling of African/Caribbean infant boys', *British Journal of Sociology of Education*, 16, (1), 75–92.

Connolly, P. (1998) *Racism, Gender Identities and Young Children*, London: Routledge.

Cooper, R. (1989) 'Modernism, postmodernism and organizational analysis: the contribution of Jacques Derrida', *Organisational Studies*, 10, 479–502.

Corsaro, W. and Molinari, L. (2000) 'Entering and observing in children's worlds: a reflection on a longitudinal ethnography of early education in Italy' in P. Christensen and A. James (eds), *Research with Children: Perspectives and Practices*, London: Falmer Press.

Culler, J. (1982) *On Deconstruction: Theory and Criticism after Structuralism*, Ithaca, NY: Cornell University Press.

Daly, M. (1978) *Gyn/Ecology: The Metaethics of Radical Feminism*, Boston, MA: Beacon Press.

Davies, B. (1989) *Frogs and Snails and Feminist Tales: Preschool Children and Gender*, Sydney: Unwin.

Davies, B. and Harre, R. (1999) 'Positioning and personhood' in R. Harre and L. van Langenhove (eds), *Positioning Theory*, Oxford: Blackwell.

Davis, J. and Tichner, J. (1986) 'Can girls build or do they choose not to? A study of girls and boys using construction materials', *Primary Teaching Studies*, 1, London: University of North London.

De Beauvoir, S. (1972) *The Second Sex*, Harmondsworth: Penguin.

Deegan, M. J. (2001) 'The Chicago School of Ethnography' in P. Atkinson, A. Coffey, S. Delamont, J. Lofland and L. Lofland (eds), *Handbook of Ethnography*, London: Sage.

Deem, R. (1980) *Schooling for Women's Work*, London: Routlege & Kegan Paul.

Deleuze, G. (1992) 'What is dispositif?', in M. Foucault, *Philosopher*, New York: Routledge.

Deleuze, G. and Guattari, F. (1987) *A Thousand Plateaus: Capitalism and Schizophrenia*, London: The Athlone Press.

Deleuze, G. and Guattari, F. (2004) *A Thousand Plateaus*, London: Continuum.

Denzin, N. and Lincoln, Y. (1995) 'Transforming qualitative research methods: is it a revolution?', *Journal of Contemporary Ethnography*, 24, (3), 349–58.

Derrida, J. (1976) *Of Grammatology* (trans. G. C. Spivak), Baltimore, MD: Johns Hopkins University Press.

Derrida, J. (1978) *Writing and Difference*, Chicago, IL: University of Chicago Press.

Derrida, J. (1981) *Positions*, (trans. A. Bass), London: Routledge & Kegan Paul.

Derrida, J. (1994) 'Deconstruction of actuality: an interview with Jacques Derrida', *Radical Philosophy*, 68, 28–41.

Derrida, J. (2002) *Postitions* (2nd edn) London: Continuum.

DfEE (England) (1997) *Excellence in Schools* (Cmnd. 3681), London: Department for Education and Employment.

Di Stafano, C. (1990) 'Dilemmas of difference' in L. Nicholson (ed.), *Feminism/Postmodernism*, London: Routledge.

Dreyfus, H. L. and Rabinow, P. (1982) *Michel Foucault: Beyond Structuralism and Hermeneutics*, Chicago, IL: University of Chicago Press.

Dwyer, C. (2000) 'Negotiating diasporic identities: young British South Asian Muslim women', *Women's Studies International Forum*, 23, (4), 475–86.

Dyer, R. (ed.) (1997) *Gays and Film*, London: British Film Institute.

Ehrlich, S. (1999) 'Communities of practice, gender, and the representation of sexual assault', *Language in Society*, 28, (2), 239–56.

Emerson, R., Fretz, R. and Shaw, L. (2001) 'Participant observation and fieldnotes' in P. Atkinson, A. Coffey, S. Delamont, J. Lofland and L. Lofland (eds), *Handbook of Ethnography*, London: Sage.

Finkelstein, N. W. and Haskins, R. (1983) 'Kindergarten children prefer same color peers', *Child Development*, 54, (2), 502–8.

Flax, J. (1990) 'Postmodernism and gender relations in feminist theory' in L. Nicholson (ed.), *Feminism/Postmodernism*, London: Routledge.

Fleer, M. (2003) 'Early childhood education as an evolving "community of practice" or as lived "social reproduction": researching the "taken for granted"', *Contemporary Issues in Early Childhood*, 4, (1), 64–79.

Foucault, M. (1972) *The Archaeology of Knowledge*, London: Tavistock.

Foucault, M. (1983) 'Why study power: the question of the subject' in H. L. Dreyfus and P. Rabinow (eds), *Beyond Structuralism and Hermeneutics: Michel Foucault*, Chicago, IL: University of Chicago Press.

Foucault, M. (1998) *The Will to Knowledge: The History of Sexuality 1*, London: Penguin.

Foucault, M. (2002) *Power: Essential Works Volume 3*, London: Penguin.

Francis, B. (2001) 'Commonality and difference in education', *International Studies in Sociology of Education*, 11, (2), 157–72.

Fraser, N. and Nicholson, L. (1990) 'Social criticism without philosophy: an encounter between feminism and postmodernism' in L. Nicholson (ed.), *Feminism/Postmodernism*, London: Routledge.

Freud, S. (1991) *The Essentials of Psychoanalysis*, London: Penguin.

Garratt, D. and Li, Y. (2005) 'The foundations of experimental/empirical research methods' in B. Somekh and C. Lewin (eds), *Research Methods in the Social Sciences*, London: Sage.

Gee, J. P. (1990) *Social Linguistics and Literacies: Ideology in Discourses*, London: Falmer.

Giddens, A. (1991) *Modernity and Self Identity: Self and Society in the Late Modern Age*, Cambridge: Polity Press.

Giroux, H. (1991) 'Democracy and the discourse of cultural difference: towards a politics of border pedagogy', *British Journal of Sociology of Education*, 12, (4), 501–19.

Goodley, D., Lawthom, R., Clough, P. and Moore, M. (2004) *Researching Life Stories: Method, Theory and Analyses in a Biographic Age*, London: RoutledgeFalmer.

Gordon, T., Holland, J. and Lahelma, E. (2001) 'Ethnographic research in educational settings' in P. Atkinson, A. Coffey, S. Delamont, J. Lofland and L. Lofland (eds), *Handbook of Ethnography*, London: Sage.

Gorrard, S., Rees, G. and Salisbury, J. (1999) 'Reappraising the apparent underachievement of boys at school', *Gender and Education*, 11, (4), 441–54.

Gorrard, S., Rees, G. and Salisbury, J. (2001) 'Investigating the patterns of differential attainment of boys and girls at school', *British Educational Research Journal*, 27, (2), 125–39.

Gould, S. (1981) *The Mismeasure of Men*, New York: W.W. Norton.

Grieshaber, S. and Cannella, G. (2001) 'From identity to identities: increasing possibilities in early childhood education' in S. Grieshaber and G. Cannella (eds),

Embracing Identities in Early Childhood Education: diversity and possibilities, New York: Teachers College Press.

Grosz, E. (1990) *Jacques Lacan: A Feminist Introduction*, London: Routledge.

Gurian, M. and Henley, P. (2001) *Boys and Girls Learn Differently! A Guide for Teachers and Parents*, San Francisco, CA: Jossey-Bass.

Habermas, J. (1985) 'Modernity: an incomplete project' in H. Foster (ed.), *Postmodern Culture*, London: Pluto Press.

Hall, S. (1992) 'The question of cultural identity' in S. Hall, D. Held and T. McGrew (eds), *Modernity and its Futures*, Cambridge: Polity Press.

Hall, S. (1997) 'The spectacle of the "other"' in S. Hall (ed.), *Representation: Cultural Representations and Signifying Practices*, London: Sage.

Hallberg, H. (1992) 'Feminist epistemology: an impossible project' in S. Hall, D. Held and T. McGrew (eds), *Modernity and its Futures*, Cambridge: Polity Press.

Hammersley, M. (2005) 'Countering the "new orthodoxy" in educational research: a response to Phil Hodkinson', *British Educational Research Journal*, 31, (2) 139–55.

Hammersley, M. and Atkinson, P. (1995): *Ethnography* (2nd edn), London: Routledge.

Hekman, S. (1990) *Gender and Knowledge*, Cambridge: Polity Press.

Henriques, J., Holloway, W., Urwin, C., Venn, C. and Walkerdine, V. (1998) *Changing the Subject* (2nd edn), London: Routledge.

Hodges, D. (1998) 'Participation as dis-identification within/in a community of practice', *Mind, Culture and Activity*, 5, (4), 272–90.

Hodkinson, P. (2004) 'Research as a form of work: expertise, community and methodological objectivity', *British Educational Research Journal*, 30, (1), 9–26.

Hodkinson, P. and Hodkinson, H. (2003) 'Individuals, communities of practice and the policy context: school teachers' learning in the workplace', *Studies in Continuing Education*, 25, (1), 3–21.

Hoff Sommers, C. (2000) *The War Against Boys: How Misguided Feminism is Harming our Young Men*, New York: Simon & Schuster.

Holmes, J. and Meyerhoff, M. (1999) 'The community of practice: theories and methodologies in language and gender research', *Language in Society*, 28, (2), 173–83.

hooks, b. (1984) *Feminist Theory: From Margin to Center*, Boston, MA: South End Press.

Jackson, C. (2003) 'Motives for "laddishness" at school: a fear of failure and fear of the "feminine"', *British Educational Research Journal*, 29, (4), 584–97.

James, A. (1999) 'Researching children's social competence' in M. Woodhead, D. Faulkner and K. Littlelton (eds), *Making Sense of Social Development*, London: Routledge.

Jones, L. (2002) 'Derrida goes to nursery school: deconstructing young children's stories', *Contemporary Issues in Early Childhood* 3 (1), 139–46.

Jones, L., Barron, I., Powell, J. and Holmes, R. (2005) 'Concluding remarks' in L. Jones, R. Holmes and J. Powell (eds), *Early Childhood Studies: A Multi-professional Perspective*, Maidenhead: Open University Press.

Jones, L. and Osgood, J. (2006) *The Fabricated Identity of Childminders*, (forthcoming).

Jordan, E. (1995) 'Fighting boys and fantasy play: the construction of masculinity in the early years of school', *Gender and Education*, 7, (1), 69–86.

Kearney, R. (1986) *Modern Movements in European Philosophy*, Manchester: Manchester University Press.

Kohlberg, L. (1984) *Psychology of Moral Development*, New York: Harper & Row.

Kowalski, K. (2003) 'The emergence of ethnic and racial attitudes in preschool-aged children', *Journal of Social Psychology*, 143, (6), 677–90.

Kowalski, K. and Lo, Y.-F. (2001) 'The influence of perceptual features, ethnic labels, and sociocultural information on the development of ethnic/racial bias in young children', *Journal of Cross-Cultural Psychology*, 32, (41), 444–55.

Kristeva, J. (1981) 'Women's time', (trans. A. Jardine) *Signs*, 7, (1).

Lacan, J. (1989) *Ecrits: A Selection*, London: Routledge.

Lather, P. (1991) *Getting Smart*, London: Routledge.

Lather, P. (1993) 'Fertile obsession: validity after post-structuralism', *Sociological Quarterly*, 34, (4), 673–93.

Lather, P. (2001) 'Postmodernism, post-structuralism and post(critical) ethnography: of ruins, aporias and angels' in P. Atkinson, A. Coffey, S. Delamont, J. Lofland and L. Lofland (eds), *Handbook of Ethnography*, London: Sage.

Lave, J. (1996) 'Teaching, as learning, in practice', *Mind, Culture, and Activity*, 3, (3), 149–64.

Lave, J. and Wenger, E. (1991) *Situated Learning: Legitimate Peripheral Participation*, Cambridge: Cambridge University Press.

Le Doeuff, M. (1991) *Hipparchia's Choice: An Essay Concerning Women, Philosophy, Etc*, Oxford: Blackwell.

Lineham, C. and McCarthy, J. (2000) 'Positioning in practice: understanding participation in the social world', *Journal for the Theory of Social Behaviour*, 30, (4), 435–53.

Lingard, B. and Douglas, P. (1999) *Men Engaging Feminisms: Profeminism, Backlashes and Schooling*, Buckingham: Open University Press.

Lorde, A. (1984) *Sister Outsider*, New York: Crossing Press.

Lugones, M. (1987) 'Playfulness, "world"-travelling and loving perception', *Hypatia* 2, (2), 3–19.

Lugones, M. and Spellman, E. (1983) 'Have we got theory for you! Feminist theory, cultural imperialism and the demand for "the woman's voice"', *Women's Studies International Forum*, 6, (6), 573–81.

Lyotard, J.-F. (1984) *The Postmodern Condition: A Report on Knowledge* (trans. G. Bennington and B. Massumi), Minneapolis, MN: University of Minnesota Press.

Mac an Ghaill, M. (1994) *The Making of Men: Masculinities, Sexualities and Schooling*, Milton Keynes: Open University Press.

MacLure, M. (2003) *Discourse in Educational and Social Research*, Buckingham: Open University Press.

MacNaughton, G. (2000) *Rethinking Gender in Early Childhood Education*, London: Paul Chapman.

MacNaughton, G. (2003) *Shaping Early Childhood*, Buckingham: Open University Press.

MacNaughton, G., Mortimer, J. and Parish, K. (1986) *Working Together: Good Practice Guidelines*, London: Greater London Council.

Mahony, P. (1985) *Schools for the Boys? Co-education Reassessed*, London: Hutchinson.

Martino, W. and Berrill, D. (2003) 'Boys, schooling and masculinities: interrogating the "Right" way to educate boys', *Educational Review*, 44, (2), 99–117.

Marx, K. and Engels, F. (1969) *Manifesto of the Communist Party* (original 1848), Moscow: Progress Publishers.

May, N. and Ruddock, J. (1983) *Sex Stereotyping and the Early Years of Schooling*, University of East Anglia: Centre for Applied Research in Education.

Maynard, T. (2001) 'The student teacher and the school community of practice: a consideration of learning as participation', *Cambridge Journal of Education*, 31, (1) 39–52.

McLennan, G. (1992) 'The enlightenment project revisited' in S. Hall, D. Held and T. McGrew (eds), *Modernity and its Futures*, Cambridge: Polity Press.

Measor, L. and Woods, P. (1991) 'Breakthroughs and blockages' in G. Walford (ed.), *Doing Educational Research*, London: Routledge.

Moi, T. (1985) *Sexual Textual Politics*, New York: Routledge.

Moraga, C. and Anzaldua, G. (1998) *This Bridge Called My Back: Writings by Radical Women of Color*, New York: Kitchen Table Press.

Morss, J. (1996) *Growing Critical: Alternatives to Developmental Psychology*, London: Routledge.

Murphy, E. and Dingwall, R. (2001) 'The ethics of ethnography' in P. Atkinson, A. Coffey, S. Delamont, J. Lofland and L. Lofland (eds), *Handbook of Ethnography*, London: Sage.

Myers, K. (2000) *Whatever Happened to Equal Opportunities in Schools?: Gender Equality Initiatives in Education*, Buckingham: Open University Press.

Nayak, A. (2006) 'After race: ethnography, race and post-race theory', *Ethnic and Racial Studies*, 29, (3), 411–30.

Nilsen, R. D. (2005) 'Searching for analytical concepts in the research process: learning from children', *Social Research Methodology*, 8, (2), 117–35.

Nye, A. (1988) *Feminist Theory and the Philosophies of Man*, New York: Routledge.

Ostermann, A. C. (2003) 'Communities of practice at work: gender, facework and the power of the *habitus* at an all-female police station and a feminist crisis intervention center in Brazil', *Discourse & Society*, 14, (4), 473–505.

Outhwaite, W. (1998) 'Realism and social science' in M. Archer, R. Bhaskar, A. Collier, T. Lawson and A. Norrie (eds), *Critical Realism: Essential Readings*, London: Routledge.

Paechter, C. (1998) *Educating the Other: Gender, Power and Schooling*, London: Falmer Press.

Paechter, C. (2003a) 'Learning masculinities and femininities: power/knowledge and legitimate peripheral participation', *Women's Studies International Forum*, 26, (6), 541–52

Paechter, C. (2003b) 'Masculinities and femininities as communities of practice', *Women's Studies International Forum*, 26, (1), 69–77.

Paechter, C. (2006) 'Reconceptualising the gendered body: learning and constructing masculinities and femininities in school', *Gender and Education*, 18, (2), 13–26.

Parker, S. (1997) *Reflective Teaching in the Postmodern World: A Manifesto for Education in Postmodernity*, Buckingham: Open University Press.

Phillips, D. C. (1993) 'Subjectivity and objectivity: an objective inquiry' in M. Hammersley (ed.), *Educational Research: Current Issues*, London: Paul Chapman.

Phinney, J. S. (1990) 'Ethnic identity in adolescents and adults: review of research', *Psychological Bulletin*, 108, (3), 499–514.

Phinney, J. S. (1996) 'When we talk about American ethnic groups, what do we mean?', *American Psychologist*, 51, (9), 918–27.

Piaget, J. (1954) *The Child's Construction of Reality*, London: Routledge & Kegan Paul.

Pignatelli, F. (1993) 'What can I do? Foucault on freedom and the question of teacher agency', *Educational Theory*, 43, (4), 411–32.

Plummer, K. (2001) 'The call of life stories in ethnographic research' in P. Atkinson, A. Coffey, S. Delamont, J. Lofland and L. Lofland (eds), *Handbook of Ethnography*, London: Sage.

Popkewitz, T. S. (1997) 'The production of reason and power: curriculum history and intellectual traditions', *Journal of Curriculum Studies*, 29, (2), 131–64.

Renold, E. (2004) ' "Other" boys: negotiating non-hegemonic masculinities in the primary school', *Gender and Education*, 16, (2), 247–66.

Rhedding-Jones, J. (2001) 'Shifting ethnicities: "native informants" and other theories from/for early childhood education', *Contemporary Issues in Early Childhood*, 2, (2), 135–56.

Rhedding-Jones, J. (2002) 'An undoing of documents and other texts: towards a critical multiculturalism in early childhood education', *Contemporary Issues in Early Childhood*, 3, (1), 90–116.

Rich, A. (1976) *Of Woman Born*, New York: Norton.

Rock, P. (2001) 'Symbolic interactionism and ethnography' in P. Atkinson, A. Coffey, S. Delamont, J. Lofland and L. Lofland (eds), *Handbook of Ethnography*, London: Sage.

Sayer, A. (1998) 'Abstraction: a realist interpretation' in M. Archer, R. Bhaskar, A. Collier, T. Lawson and A. Norrie (eds), *A Critical Realism: Essential Readings*, London: Routledge.

Schaffer, R. (1996) *Social Development*, Oxford: Blackwell.

Scheurich, J. (1997) *Research Methods in the Postmodern*, London: RoutledgeFalmer.

Schön, D. A. (1983) *The Reflective Practitioner*, London: Temple Smith.

Scott, D. and Usher, R. (1991) *Researching Education: Data, Methods and Theory in Educational Enquiry*, London: Cassell.

Scott, M. (1980) 'Teach her a lesson: sexist curriculum in patriarchal education' in D. Spender and E. Sarah (eds), *Learning to Lose: Sexism and Education*, London: The Women's Press.

Shaffir, W. (1999) 'Doing ethnography', *Journal of Contemporary Ethnography*, 28, (6), 676–86.

Sharpe, S. (1976) *Just Like a Girl: How Girls Learn to be Women*, London: Penguin.

Short, G. (1999) 'Children's grasp of controversial issues' in M. Woodhead, D. Faulkner and K. Littleton (eds), *Making Sense of Social Development*, London: Routledge.

Siegel, H. (1988) *Educating Reason,* London: Routledge & Kegan Paul.

Sim, S. (1996) 'Structuralism and poststructuralism' in O. Hanfling (ed.), *Philosophical Aesthetics: An Introduction,* Milton Keynes: Open University Press.

Skattebol, J. (2005) 'Insider/outsider belongings: traversing the borders of whiteness in early childhood', *Contemporary Issues in Early Childhood,* 6, (2), 189–203.

Skeggs, B. (1997) *Formations of Class and Gender: Becoming Respectable,* London: Sage.

Skelton, C. (1996) 'Learning to be "Tough": the fostering of maleness in one primary school', *Gender and Education,* 8, (2), 185–98.

Skelton, C. and Hall, E. (2001) *The Development of Gender Roles in Young Children: A Review of Policies and Literature,* Manchester: Equal Opportunities Commission.

Smith, B. (1983) *Home Girls: A Black Feminist Anthology,* New York: Kitchen Table Press.

Smith, J. K. (1989) *The Nature of Social and Educational Enquiry: Empiricism versus Interpretation,* Norwood, NJ: Ablex.

Sondergaard, D. M. (2002) 'Theorizing subjectivity: contesting the monopoly of psychoanalysis', *Feminism and Psychology,* 12, (4), 445–54.

Spencer, J. (2001) 'Ethnography after postmodernism' in P. Atkinson, A. Coffey, S. Delamont, J. Lofland and L. Lofland (eds), *Handbook of Ethnography,* London: Sage.

Spender, D. (1982) *Invisible Women,* London: Writers and Readers.

Spivak, G. (1980) 'Revolutions that have as yet no model' in D. Landry and G. McLean (eds), *The Spivak Reader,* London: Routledge.

Stanton, W. (1960) *The Leopard's Spots: Scientific Attitudes Towards Race in America 1815–59,* Chicago, IL: University of Chicago Press.

Stapleton, K. (2001) 'Constructing a feminist identity:

discourse and the community of practice', *Feminism and Psychology*, 11, (4), 459–91.

Stapleton, K. (2003) 'Gender and swearing: a community practice', *Women and Language*, 26, (2), 22–33.

Stronach, I. and MacLure, M. (1997) *Educational Research Undone: The Postmodern Embrace*, Buckingham: Open University Press.

Swain, J. (2004) 'The resources and strategies that 10–11-year-old boys use to construct masculinities in the school', *British Educational Research Journal*, 30, (1), 167–85.

Taylor, M. (1987) 'Descartes, Nietzsche and the search for the unsayable', *New York Times Book Review*, 1 February, 3.

Thompson, K. (1992) 'Social pluralism and post-modernity' in S. Hall, D. Held and T. McGrew (eds), *Modernity and its Futures*, Cambridge: Polity Press.

Van Maanen, J. (1988) *Tales of the Field: On Writing Ethnography*, London: University of Chicago Press.

Verkuyten, M. (2005) *The Social Psychology of Ethnic Identity*, Hove: Psychology Press.

Walkerdine, V. (1981) 'Sex, power and pedagogy', *Screen*, 38, 14–21.

Walkerdine, V. (1984) 'Developmental psychology and the child-centred pedagogy: the Insertion of Piaget into early education' in J. Henriques, W. Holloway, C. Urwin and V. Walkerdine (eds), *Changing the Subject*, London: Methuen.

Warrington, M. and Younger, M. (2000) 'The other side of the gender gap', *Gender and Education*, 12, (4), 493–508.

Weedon, C. (1999) *Feminism, Theory and the Politics of Difference*, Oxford: Blackwell.

Weiler, K. (1988) *Women Teaching for Change: Gender, Class and Power*, South Hadley, MA: Bergin & Harvey.

Wenger, E. (1998) *Communities of Practice: Learning,*

Meaning and Identity, Cambridge: Cambridge University Press.

Wollstonecraft, M. (1975) *A Vindication of the Rights of Woman* (original 1792), Harmondsworth: Penguin.

Yelland, G. (ed.) (1998) *Gender in Early Childhood*, London: RoutledgeFalmer.

Yelland, G. (2005) *Critical Issues in Early Childhood Education*, Maidenhead: Open University Press.

Yelland, N. and Grieshaber, S. (1998) 'Blurring the edges' in N. Yelland (ed.), *Gender in Early Childhood*, London: Routledge.

Younger, M. and Warrington, M. with Gray, J., Ruddock, J., McLellan, R., Bearne, E., Kershner, R. and Bricheno, P. (2005) *Raising Boys' Achievement*, London: Norwich, HMSO.

Index

Index